The Impact of Federal Antipoverty Policies

Charles Brecher
foreword by
Eli Ginzberg

Conservation of Human Resources Studies—
Columbia University

The Praeger Special Studies program—
utilizing the most modern and efficient book
production techniques and a selective
worldwide distribution network—makes
available to the academic, government, and
business communities significant, timely
research in U.S. and international economic, social, and political development.

The Impact of Federal Antipoverty Policies

PRAEGER SPECIAL STUDIES IN U.S. ECONOMIC, SOCIAL, AND POLITICAL ISSUES

Praeger Publishers   New York   Washington   London

Library of Congress Cataloging in Publication Data

Brecher, Charles.
  The impact of Federal antipoverty policies.

  (Conservation of human resources studies)
(Praeger special studies in U. S. economic, social,
and political issues)
  Bibliography: p.
  1. Economic assistance, Domestic—United States—
Case studies. I. Title. II. Series: Conservation of
human resources studies.
HC110. P63B7   338. 973   73-5227

Publ. 1100 |5|20|74

PRAEGER PUBLISHERS
111 Fourth Avenue, New York, N.Y. 10003, U.S.A.
5, Cromwell Place, London SW7 2JL, England

Published in the United States of America in 1973
by Praeger Publishers, Inc.

Printed in the United States of America

The Conservation of Human Resources Project, Columbia University, is an interdisciplinary research group now in its fourth decade of working in the field of human resources and manpower. Its investigations cover a broad spectrum with primary emphasis on the role of human resources in the economic development of the United States but including also other advanced economies and the developing world. In recent years the Conservation Project has increasingly focused on metropolitan labor markets. The Project also engages in research in health policy issues. Professor Eli Ginzberg, 525 Uris, Columbia University, New York, New York 10027, is director of the Project.

ACKNOWLEDGMENTS

This book represents the merger of two research interests. One derives from my studies of manpower problems at the Conservation of Human Resources Project, Columbia University. Dr. Eli Ginzberg, the Project's director, stimulated my interest in federal manpower programs, and his enlightened attitude as an employer permitted me to pursue the topic in my chosen fashion. He read the manuscript carefully and made comments that provided the basis for substantial improvements.

The other research interest represented in this book derives from my studies at the Political Science Program of the Graduate School of the City University of New York. While completing my doctoral studies there I developed an interest in the political dimensions of antipoverty programs. Professors Dennis Palumbo and Marilyn Gittell, who served as my dissertation advisers, encouraged this aspect of my work, and much of the research for my doctoral dissertation is embodied in this book.

This research effort could not have been completed without the cooperation of officials at the Manpower Administration, U. S. Department of Labor, and at the Office of Economic Opportunity. The research offices of both agencies made available to me contract studies they had commissioned.

Although this book could not have been completed without the assistance of each of the individuals mentioned, the responsibility for any errors of fact or judgment is entirely mine.

This is a useful and insightful book. Dr. Brecher set himself two tasks and carried each through to a satisfactory conclusion. As a political scientist directly involved in manpower studies (see his *Upgrading Blue Collar and Service Workers* [Baltimore: The Johns Hopkins Press, 1972]), Brecher postulated that it would be worthwhile to analyze the efficacy of federal antipoverty programs. Specifically, he directed his inquiries to two dimensions of the efforts of the Kennedy and Johnson administrations in the 1960s. His first analysis is focused on the Manpower Development and Training Act (1962) and its subsequent amendments, which transformed the act into an antipoverty program. The MDTA, in the author's terminology, is a classic service program in which federal funds are directed to improving the economic lot of the seriously disadvantaged by enabling them to increase their skills and improve their employability through training.

His second inquiry is focused on the Economic Opportunity Act (EOA, 1964), particularly Title II, which provides federal funding for the establishment and operation of community action agencies, which attempt to assist persons living in poverty to organize in order to exercise more leverage on local institutions so that they become more responsive to the needs and demands of the low-income population. Brecher defines this approach as the "political strategy," to distinguish it from the "service strategy" of MDTA.

Specifically, the author attempts to determine the extent to which these two governmental efforts to help the disadvantaged have been successful. These are important questions, not only because of the public's need to know whether its dollars have been constructively used but also because the vitality of a democracy depends on feedback information. Unless the programs and policies that the legislature passes and the executive implements are assessed and the results acted upon, the gap between goals and outcomes cannot be narrowed. No single effort at political reform, no matter how wide ranging, can by itself be completely responsive to the needs and demands of the citizenry. The elimination of disabilities and the broadening of options can come about only as the electorate, after assessing earlier efforts at reforms, decides to increase and intensify these efforts or start off in a new direction.

Dr. Brecher's assessment of the effectiveness of the Manpower Training and Development Act and Title II of the Economic Opportunity Act in enhancing the economic and political power of the poor is an early exploration of program and policy evaluation that should have increasing interest for both scholars and politicians.

Brecher tells us about his frustration when he was unable to find adequate data with which to assess these two programs. The Department of Labor does not report trainees by their poverty status. Consequently, Brecher was forced to use trainee characteristics that were correlates of poverty.

Futhermore, the author was unable to find reliable studies that would permit him to compare the posttraining earnings with those of comparable members of the labor force who had not participated in training programs. As Brecher states, unless studies of experimental and control groups are carefully designed and implemented, the findings should not be used for policy guidance. In the author's judgment, there does not exist, a decade after the establishment of MDTA, a single large-scale study that meets the criteria of survey research.

Despite inadequate data and follow-up studies, Brecher demonstrates considerable ingenuity in going around these roadblocks in assessing the responsiveness of MDTA to the needs of the poverty population. The statistical information furnished by the U.S. Department of Labor in the annual *Manpower Report of the President* enables Brecher to reach the following conclusions about the service strategy.

Institutional training under MDTA after 1965 was highly responsive to the seriously disadvantaged: A high proportion, almost 75 percent, of all enrollees came from low-income families and were otherwise disadvantaged; it is presumed that they were living in poverty. The opposite applied to those who entered on-the-job training; the data suggest more creaming. The analysis is complicated by the fact that after 1968, on-the-job training was increasingly carried out through Job Opportunities in the Business Sector (JOBS), which included two parallel efforts: one voluntary, the other with federal subsidies. The business leaders who spearheaded these efforts issued many press releases but little hard data about progress in meeting the target of adding 500,000 disadvantaged persons to their payrolls by 1971. Since the "voluntary" hiring of a disadvantaged person is a matter of employer discretion in reporting and since the target included both voluntary and contract hires, the statistical picture is badly blurred, and all conclusions must be treated as approximations. Brecher notes that in 1969-71 employers were unable to use all the funds allocated by the Department of Labor for the contract portion of JOBS. This failure of the private sector to use all the appropriated funds leads Brecher to conclude that this facet of the MDTA program must be adjudged a partial failure. If the aim of the program was to provide good jobs for the disadvantaged through the lubricant of a governmental subsidy to the employer to cover the additional costs of training and support services and if employers failed to make adequate training opportunities available, only one conclusion can be drawn: The program failed to accomplish its stated goals.

Although Brecher gives institutional training under MDTA a good mark because a high proportion of its enrollees were disadvantaged persons, he does not see it as a successful service program for the poverty population. As he correctly notes, training is not an end in itself; it must be assessed in terms of whether it leads the completer to a better job and higher wages. And on this crucial issue the data base was so inadequate that the author was unable to reach a firm conclusion.

Accordingly, Brecher concludes that the service strategy, which was aimed at helping the poverty population through institutional and on-the-job training, can be adjudged at best to have been only partially successful. Much of the money that Congress appropriated did not go to the seriously disadvantaged but to other unemployed and underemployed workers. Moreover, the money that Congress allocated to help the disadvantaged was not put fully to use; the business community did not create an adequate number of on-the-job training slots. Most importantly, there is no unequivocal evidence that entrance into and successful completion of a training program ensured that the disadvantaged person would get and hold a job that would pay him more than he had earned in the past.

Before assessing the political strategy, Brecher is careful to help the reader recognize the complex problems inherent in the fact that the thousand or more community action agencies had set themselves differing objectives. Organizing the poor to enhance their political power was by no means a primary or even secondary goal for many of them. Many CAAs were service or employment oriented. Nevertheless, one can postulate that every CAA that achieved any order of success in providing services or expanding employment opportunities for the poor must have contributed *inter alia* to enhancing the polical power of the poverty population.

In pursuing his inquiry into the extent to which the political strategy of the poverty approach subsumed under Title II of the Economic Opportunity Act—maximum feasible participation of the poor—proved successful, Brecher found a valuable source. The Office of Economic Opportunity (OEO) had contracted with two consulting firms to study a large number of CAAs specifically from this vantage point—namely, had they been successful in organizing the poor to play a larger role in the decision-making process with respect to the uses to which federal funds for the poor were expended and in exerting leverage on the local power structure, in both government and the voluntary sector, to be more responsive to the demands of the poor?

Brecher's careful reading and analysis of these evaluation reports led him to a cautious, though not negative, conclusion. He gives the political strategy a low but passing mark. He recognized that it takes time and experience to organize the poor, for local leaders to emerge, and for them to develop the range of skills required to advance the interests of their constituents. And as Brecher makes clear, time was not on the side of the CAAs. At both federal and local levels, once the political leadership recognized the potential threat to their power in Title II, it moved energetically through legislation, administration, and informal agreements to throw up roadblocks in front of the CAAs.

Brecher goes through an interesting analysis of the extent to which different CAAs, with different styles, operating in different urban environments, were able to enhance the political power of the poor. He demonstrates conclusively that the most strident and agressive CAAs were not necessarily the most successful and that success depended as much or more on the receptiveness or hostility of the community as on their own strategies and tactics.

On the basis of his analysis, Brecher concludes that with respect to both the service and the political strategies, the federal government's efforts in the l960s on behalf of the poor had limited success.

Brecher's finding of limited success in federal antipoverty efforts must be placed in the context of the shortcomings inherent in all policy evaluations. Evaluations are necessarily limited in their sensitivity to the scale of federal policy, the time required for institution building, the necessity of forging political coalitions, the importance of changes in the macro-environment, and the significance of secondary consequences. A few words about each.

With respect to the level of federal funding, we must note that manpower training started as a small, temporary program to which the states were expected to contribute. It took the larger part of a decade to bring the total outlay to $1.5 billion annually. In the late 1960s, the Department of Labor staff made an estimate that the universe of persons who could profit from manpower training and related services was of the order of 12 million, while current legislation made limited opportunities available for about 1 million. A major consequence of this gap between the need for and the availability of manpower services was the pressures in Congress and in the administration to spread the available dollars over the widest possible constituency. As a result, many training and support services were too thin to make a significant difference in the employment and income of the enrollees. The simple fact is that some enrollees, including some from among the poverty population, who were able to enter and complete a serious course, such as in refrigerator repair or in practical-nurse's training, were likely to find a good job upon completion, one that enabled them to enjoy a significant increase in income. *Per contra,* many were enrolled in short programs that did not provide them with additional skill or otherwise improve their employability. Social science is concerned with averages, but new programs are often characterized by successes and failures that averaging obscures.

A second problem in policy evaluation that bears on this study is the amount of time that must pass before an investigator is able to assess the effectiveness of new legislation that is geared to institution building or re-structuring. We are an impatient people who believe that once we decide to do something, even something as complex as the eradication of poverty, the results should be immediately or shortly visible. But societal structures are firmly rooted, and they do not yield readily to every force, not even to money plus enthusiasm plus dedication. It requires long and hard work to alter the relative positions of groups in the marketplace and in the political arena. Those who hold the better jobs with preferred career opportunities as well as those among the decision-makers or allied to them will not readily yield their places to the challengers. In fact they are likely to fight and fight hard to maintain the advantages they have acquired, often as a result of years of concentrated effort.

Admittedly, there is a dilemma here. If students wait before reviewing the results of new legislation and administrative actions, they may be unable to provide the authorities and the public with useful feedback in time about how the changes and innovations are working. And if appraisals are undertaken too soon after the new structures are in place, their effectiveness cannot be properly gauged. The only escape from this dilemma is to proceed with analysis as soon as requisite information becomes available but to recognize, as Dr. Brecher does, that judgments reached must be viewed as tentative, not definitive, because of foreshortened perspective.

An even more difficult question is the selection of criteria for assessing MDTA. One focus is the proportion of the total enrollees who come from the poverty population, a measure justified by the post-1965 legislative and administrative commitments to concentrate on assisting the seriously disadvantaged. While the goals announced by policy-makers are generally the best guide to criteria for evaluation, in this case it is important to note other tactical considerations. It is by no means clear that restricting enrollees in training programs to the seriously disadvantaged is sound policy from any of the following vantages: the continuing support of Congress with respect to funding; effectiveness in the design and operation of a broad training program; reasonable success in placing the completers in desirable jobs. Those at the end of the income scale do not carry much political clout. It is much easier therefore to secure and maintain congressional support for measures that are geared to helping a much wider segment of the population. Admittedly, more broadly focused programs run the risk that the seriously disadvantaged will not receive more than a part of the new resources and that a significant proportion will go to people who do not need it as much. But the poverty population will benefit more if it can attract half of a program's resources over a period of 5 or 10 years than if it receives all of them for 2 or 3 years.

There are other grounds for questioning the wisdom of limiting a manpower training effort to the seriously handicapped. It is difficult to design effective training programs, and it is at least as difficult to elicit and maintain strong employer involvement in the placement and promotion of completers. Once again, it may be the better part of a long-term strategy to broaden the population group so that the seriously disadvantaged are not the sole or even primary beneficiaries.

Finally, no efforts at intervention, such as MDTA and Title II of EOA, can be studied without close attention to the changes in the macro-environment, both economic and political. On-the-job training may be successful in a tight labor market such as prevailed in the late 1960s, but it may be doomed to frustration and failure in a loose labor market such as existed in 1970-71, especially in areas of the country where the unemployment rate moved toward 10 percent or even higher. Employers will not add new workers at a time when they are forced to release old workers. Similarly, maximum feasible participation of the poor has more prospect of proving successful in a period of political reform in which the president assumes leadership than in a period when the public's stance is unresponsive to the challenges of the poor and the president is committed to stabilizing the political environment.

It would be unfair to Dr. Brecher to read these dicta relating to program scale, institutional building, the need for political coalitions, and the importance of the macro-environment on intervention outcomes as serious criticisms of his efforts and accomplishments. His handling of the inherent problems of evaluation was determined by the state of the art, and he did admirably in finding his way between research and policy. He carried out his inquiry in the face of inadequate data, and his findings and conclusions are balanced and insightful.

It is not to disparage his effort that these last pages have called attention to additional complexities and ramifications embedded in our society that limit all scientifically based evaluations of social action. For better or worse, we are forced to reach judgments about the efficacy and equity of social programs in the absence of valid cost-benefit studies. In a democratic society, politicians, not scholars, must bear the responsibility for guiding the destiny of the republic, but they should be responsive to the work of social scientists, who represent an informed constituency.

CONTENTS

LIST OF TABLES AND CHARTS

The Impact of Federal Antipoverty Policies

1

POLICY ANALYSIS
AND POLITICAL SCIENCE

POLICY AND THE POLITICAL SYSTEM

The study of public policy is not a new concern of political science. It is usually undertaken in relation to the systems framework presented by David Easton for analyzing political life.[1] This model postulates a political system functioning in the context of various intra- and extra-societal characteristics and that converts inputs (supports and demands) arising from this environment into outputs. These outputs affect the internal and external characteristics of the society and thus have a feedback effect upon the inputs.

Studies of public policy by political scientists deal with two types of relationships within this model. One group of studies deals with the effects of the economic and cultural environment and/or the structural characteristics of the political system on policy outcomes (outputs). In this context policy decisions are viewed as a dependent variable produced or explained by specified independent societal characteristics. The second type of study views the policy decision itself an an independent variable and studies its effects. In terms of Easton's model, these inquiries are directed to the impact of policy outcomes on the environment and the associated feedback effects.

Studies in the first group vary in their degree of theoretical and methodological sophistication. One large body of literature focuses on the process through which decisions are made. Many of these studies fall into what might be called the "politics of . . . " tradition. Examples that come to mind are Robert Connery's *The Politics of Mental Health*, John Donovan's *The Politics of Poverty*, and Michael Armacost's *The Politics of Weapons*

Innovatiation. [2] These and other similar works, which may or may not use the same phraseology in their titles, focus on a particular piece of legislation or set of administrative decisions such as the Community Mental Health Act, the Economic Opportunity Act, or the production of a weapon system. They analyze the impact of political factors such as interest-group positions and activities or bureaucratic postures and processes on the formulation or implementation of public policy. In some cases these studies are related, either approvingly or disapprovingly, to the broader pluralistic and interest-group conceptions of policy formulation characteristic of the discipline.[3] However, all too frequently these studies provide only historical evidence and interpretations lacking relevance to broader theoretical problems.

Another body of literature concerned with policy as a dependent variable utilizes the expenditure patterns of American states and cities to test statistically hypotheses regarding the relative importance of cultural, economic, and political variables in the determination of public policy. Such studies have provided evidence both to support and contradict the hypothesized relationship between "political ethos" and local governmental structures and policy outcomes.[4] With respect to policies at the level of state governments Thomas Dye and Richard Dawson and James Robinson have argued that levels of economic development[5] and the distribution of income[6] are the critical factors in determining many policy outcomes. Dye has summarized the general conclusions of this type of research as follows:

> Economic development shapes both political systems and policy outcomes, and most of the association that occurs between system characteristics and policy outcomes can be attributed to the influence of economic development. Differences in the policy choices of states with different types of political systems turn out to be largely a product of differing socioeconomic levels rather than a direct product of political variables. Levels of urbanization, industrialization, income and education appear to be more influential in shaping policy outcomes than political system characteristics.[7]

More recent research has challenged this general finding on theoretical and methodological grounds and because "we have been too simple-minded in our measurement of 'politics' and 'policy'."[8] The findings of subsequent studies have been summarized as follows:

> Our findings show that different social and economic characteristics have different relevance for policies, and their relevance varies between substantive areas of policy. Futhermore, central features of state politics are important for some policies, even when socioeconomic variation is controlled.[9]

2

The second type of policy analyses, that concerned with the impact of policy outcomes on the environment and the consequent feedback effect, has not been prominent in the literature of political science, but it has been recurrent. Harold Lasswell's early work *Politics: Who Gets What, When and How*[10] demonstrated a concern with the distribution of government outputs among the body politic, and in a 1960 essay he stressed the need for social scientists to explore the effectiveness of different policy alternatives in achieving specified goals.[11]

More recently as an outgrowth of the comparative study of state expenditures, Sharkansky has begun to study the actual outputs and impact of policy decisions. He distinguishes between public policy (action taken by government), policy outputs (service levels affected by policy decisions), and policy impacts (the effect that service has on a population).[12] Empirical analysis in Georgia found that policy decisions such as larger public expenditure levels did not translate directly into higher outputs or service levels, but no research was conducted on policy impacts. However, the lack of empirical work does not mean such research could not be fruitful. In discussing future trends in the discipline Sharkansky has argued that "another trend that is likely to continue is the concern with the results (the outputs, outcomes, impacts or effects) of specific policies . . . . There is nothing in the character of political science to keep its best practitioners from studying these kinds of problems. To keep the faith as social scientists, we need only base our conclusions on empirical evidence and clear standards."[13]

In a related development Kenneth Dolbeare has argued that "the systematic empirical tracing of the tangible consequences of policy within the society" will constitute the "soul of the post-behavioral revolution" in the discipline of political science.[14] Dolbeare and James Davis have already undertaken an analysis with the above objective dealing with the American Selective Service System.[15]

Davis and Dolbeare have identified what they consider to be the key issues to be dealt with in an analysis of public policy outcomes:

> By taking policy as the focus of our inquiry, rather than as the dependent product of decision-making activity, we hope to indicate some possibilities of a policy-oriented approach to the study of politics . . . . We seek to define the consequences of present conscription policies in more comprehensive fashion by asking such questions as: What happens to whom by virtue of these policies? What social and economic implications do their effects carry? To what extent are the stated goals of these policies actually realized? What would be the consequences of instituting alternative policies?[16]

These may be considered the important issues to be dealt with in a study of the impact of policy decisions.

In sum, the subfield of political science concerned with policy analysis provides for two major approaches. Policy may be viewed as a dependent variable with research aimed at isolating the determinants of decisions, or policy may be viewed as an independent variable with research aimed at tracing the impact of decisions. In recent years the first approach has prevailed, but the second is presently assigned increasing significance.

DESIGN OF THE STUDY

This study will focus on the impact of two alternative policies designed to deal with the problem of poverty in American society. The two policies, which may conveniently be labeled the "political strategy" and the "service strategy," will be defined in some detail in Chapter 2. The central concern will be the effect of the policies upon a target population—the poor. It therefore falls into the second category of policy analyses. We are asking how policy decisions made by government affect selected groups. The precise methods and criteria to be used in tracing the policy consequences will be discussed in Chapter 4.

Poverty policies usually are studied as dependent rather than as independent variables. The "politics of . . . " tradition is represented in studies by Donovan and by Sundquist[17] and in portions of works by Levitan and by Moynihan.[18] Peter Eisinger's study of six community action groups in New York City found that the quality of leadership—that is, the personality of the director—was the most important factor in determining the policy or strategy pursued by a neighborhood antipoverty agency.[19] A systematic study relating economic and political characteristics of the 50 states to their poverty (Community Action Program) expenditures has been completed by Joseph Cepuran.[20] David Greenstone and Paul Peterson have explored the effect of "machine" and "reformed" political systems on the implementation of poverty programs in four large American cities.[21] Thus, political scientists have begun to explore the factors shaping the nature and magnitude of antipoverty activity in the United States.

To date, little work has been done in tracing the consequences of antipoverty policy decisions. This study is an effort to understand the impact of antipoverty policies on the economic and political characteristics of American society. The study consists of the following parts. The remainder of this chapter considers some of the criticisms of Easton's model and their relevance to this study. Chapter 2 outlines the development and nature of the problem of poverty in the United States and describes two different policies or strategies aimed at dealing with it. Next, an effort is made to identify particular federal programs with each of these strategies by examining their legislative history and substantive provisions (Chapter 3). The fourth chapter is devoted to the specification of criteria to judge the impact of the two alternative policies and a discussion of the difficulties inherent in such research. The major part of the study is the detailed analysis of the impacts of the two selected programs—the Manpower Development and Training Act (Chapter 5) and the Economic Opportunity Act (Chapter 6). The concluding chapter builds on the findings with respect to the selected programs to speculate about the likely future consequences of implementation on a broader scale of the two antipoverty strategies and analyzes the specific findings in relation to the general systems model of policy decisions and impacts.

CRITICISMS OF THE SYSTEMS MODEL

The general systems model elaborated by Easton has been subject to criticism on the grounds that certain biases and shortcomings are inherent in any research using this framework. It is important to consider these criticisms and their revelance to the present study.

Actually, criticism has not been directed exclusively or explicitly at Easton's theory but rather has been directed at a school of thought often called behavioralism. The critics do not always specify the boundaries or identifying characteristics of the school and sometimes prefer to define it by referring to a body of literature authored by certain prominent political scientists. For example, the editors of a recent collection of critical essays introduce the volume by referring to "the various behavioralist methods" and listing Robert Dahl, David Easton, Harold Lasswell, Richard Snyder, Seymour Lipset, Gabriel Almond, Anthony Downs, William Riker, and David Truman as "those most frequently discussed."[22] As this rather diverse list indicates, the criticism reflects not exclusively on Easton's model but rather expresses a general dissatisfaction with the recent course of political science. Hence it is important to identify those aspects of the criticisms that may apply specifically to the framework chosen for this study.

The main points of the critics have been summarized by Charles McCoy as follows: "These authors find the professional writings of the behavioralists characterized by conservatism, a fear of popular democracy and an avoidance of vital political issues."[23] Each of these three points is worthy of discussion.

The avoidance of critical issues has been tersely described by Christian Bay: "A growing and now indeed a predominant proportion of leading American political scientists, the behavioralists, have become determined to achieve science. Yet in the process many of them remain open to the charge

5

of strenuously avoiding that dangerous subject, politics."[24] In its simplest form this is a charge of not pursuing those aspects of the political system that the critics consider "relevant"—civil rights, the defense establishment, and so on.

There is a twofold defense against this line of criticism. First, it is simply not true that empirically oriented political scientists have ignored these important subjects. A list of recent studies by prominent "behavioralists" might include Thomas Dye's *The Politics of Equality* (racism) or Bruce Russett's *What Price Vigilance?* (militarism).[25] These books serve only as examples of the fact that behavioral techniques and models have been applied to a variety of topics, including "relevant" ones. Second, even if it could be demonstrated that a disproportionately small share of empirical research has been directed to such topics, this fact could not be attributed to the nature of the systems model. There is nothing in the nature of the model that indicates that research be directed to some areas and not others. Rather it functions as a "general" model applicable to a wide variety of topics.

This latter point is the basis for a more serious variant of the "relevance argument." The behavioral approach and Easton's model provide no criteria for the selection of problems for investigation. With respect to policy analysis the model provides no reason to study housing policy or antipoverty programs rather than educational policy or foreign policy. Bay has argued that political science ought to include a theory that can guide the investigator to important problems: "My principal concern is to argue for a more pressing need; an intellectually more defensible and a politically more responsible theoretical framework for guiding and interpreting our empirical work, a theory that would give more meaning to our research, even at the expense of reducing its conceptual and operational neatness."[26] He has begun to develop such a theory based on the concept of common fundamental human needs:

> The burden of this paper, then, is to plead for an expansion and a more systematic articulation of the psychological and the normative perspectives of political behavior research. I propose as a normative basis the proposition that politics exists for the purpose of progressively removing the most stultifying obstacles to a free human development, with priority for those individuals who are most severely oppressed; as Harrington points out with respect to the poverty-stricken in the United States they are also the least articulate and the least likely to achieve redress by way of the ordinary democratic process.[27]

The signficant point for this investigation is that while the model provides no basis for selecting topics, this does not detract from its utility in analyzing any topic that might be selected. With respect to this research, the subject of antipoverty policies would appear to be a priority topic based on Bay's criteria.

The second major shortcoming suggested by the behavioralists' critics is the "fear of popular democracy." This criticism is generally aimed at the pluralists' interpretation of American politics, which is sometimes characterized as "the theory of democratic elitism."[28] Critics generally do not dispute the empirical finding that relatively few citizens participate actively in American politics. Rather they say of the pluralists:

> They have also shown themselves to be not unhappy about these results of their empirical research. They are opposed to any massive extension of democratic participation in the political process. They favor the maintenance of the present low level of citizenship involvement and this they justify . . . partly on the grounds that popular democracy is unmanageable and chaotic.[29]

Two specific criticisms follow from this general observation. First it is argued that political scientists ought not accept as necessary or inevitable the frequently discovered real-life situation of limited participation and, moreover, that this situation should not be granted the title "democracy." Peter Bachrach has summarized the controversy over the allegedly inherent limitations on participation and the consequences for a definition of democracy:

> It does not necessarily follow that because a political criterion cannot be fulfilled it should therefore be discarded for all practical purposes. I see no reason a principle, serving both as an ideal to strive for and a standard for judging the progress of a political system toward the achivement of that ideal, must be realizable in practice to perform its function. Of course, an unrealizable doctrine, political or religious, can lead to cynicism, but on the other hand it may be a valuable guide and a spur to a more humane society. Dahl asserts that the utopian nature of the principle of equality of political power breeds cynicism; but Roland Pennock asserts equally strongly that although it may not be fulfilled in practice, as an integral part of the democratic ideal, it has been effective in pushing the democratic reality in the direction of equality not only of access to power but also equality in the exercise of power. Where the truth lies between these conflicting appraisals is a question of judgment based upon the evidence—for surely relatively unsupported assertions one way or the other are not sufficient to dispose of the matter.[30]

7

The potential limits of political participation remain to be empirically determined, and adjustment of the definitional criteria for democracy to the present situation may serve to justify and perpetuate limited participation. Maintenance of higher definitional standards may spur expanded participation.

The second specific criticism resulting from the "fear of popular democracy" is a disregard for the contribution of mass movements as a threat to the stability and efficiency of the political system. Jack Walker has suggested that because the elitist theory disregards or distrusts mass movements it "has served as an inadequate guide to empirical research," and consequently, "little attention has been directed to the great social movements which have marked American society in the last one hundred years."[31]

This second criticism prompts the question, Does Easton's general systems model preclude the inclusion of mass phenomenon in the analysis of policy formulation? In his explication of the model Easton explicitly recognizes that demands may be voiced in a great variety of forms:

> It matters little whether the demand so stated has been voiced to a friend over cocktails, or to a fellow worker between bites of a sandwich on the end of an I-beam, to fellow sufferers before a meeting of the local rate payers association, or as a complaint, in a traditional society to a neighboring hawker at a bazaar. Nor does it matter whether the demand has been uttered in public to rouse popular support or in secret to get the ear of an effective official or powerful person. It may be voiced by the ordinary member of a political system, by an eminent political leader in the name of an interest group or political party, or even a dictator. Where it is voiced, who articulates it, who hears it, how widely it is diffused are all matters of signal importance for the future stages of the demand's career. But before it can have a future it must have a present beginning.[32]

However, as indicated in the above passage, not all demands are equally likely to result in outputs. While Easton recognizes that demands may be voiced in popular movements, he stresses that all demands cannot be acted upon, and therefore mechanisms evolve to filter out demands. The individuals whose role it is to select demands for the system are referred to as "gatekeepers," primarily party leaders and interest group officials. Easton recognizes the possibility of individuals processing their own demands but stresses the critical role of gatekeepers:

> To some minimal extent then, especially in a democracy in which conditions encourage popular interest rather than apathy, each

person is his own converter. But there are no data as yet that would permit us to hazard a guess as to the proportion of wants that are converted at the hands of general members, natural spokesmen of this sort, who occupy no special or clearly differentiated role as converter of wants. However little data we may have of the extent to which they contribute to the conversion of wants, there can at least be much less doubt that a very considerable amount of this activity is performed by others, namely by those who do hold well-defined political roles such as that of opinion leader, politician, legislator, or administrator or by organizations such as an interest group, legislature, political party or newspaper.[33]

While Easton emphasizes the role of gatekeepers, it is not true that his model precludes analysis of mass movements and their impact on the political process. In fact, Easton recognizes the possibility of by-passing the gatekeepers and deals with this phenomenon explicitly. He calls demands that are processed in this fashion "unmediated inputs" and describes them as follows:

Unmediated demands will normally reflect popular responses to special situations of distress, emergency or catastrophe, a common reaction to similar conditions that leads to the contagious and widespread popular conversion of wants almost instantaneously. The want is transmitted as a demand directly from its holders to the authorities without formal or informal intermediaries.

In the United States such a conversion took place at the end of World War II when a spontaneous grass-roots movement arose around the feeling that the government ought to "bring the boys back home." Swift decisions were taken in the wake of this popular outcry; the want was almost instantaneously transformed into a demand and soon thereafter into an output . . . .

Genuinely spontaneous grass-roots movements are quite extraordinary but they do represent one kind of conversion of wants in which, at the very least, the gatekeeping kind of regulation is minimal.[34]

As the above passages indicate, Easton's model does stress the significance of interest groups and similar organizations (gatekeepers) in the policy process, and this bias may account for the deemphasis of mass movements in pluralist writings. However, the model does take into account the existence of popular movements (unmediated inputs), and the paucity of empirical work on this phenomenon is more an oversight on the part of researchers than a shortcoming of the model.

The third major criticism is that of "conservatism." It is argued that a systems model is biased toward the establishment of an equilibrium that results in the maintenance of the political status quo. James Petras refers to the "school of stabilizing equiliberalism or simply the 'equiliberals'." He describes this group as follows: "The prime value concept underlying the work of all equiliberals is stability, the maintenance of the ongoing system. The method of balancing describes the pairing off of opposite effects or attitudes which negate each other and lead to the continuation of the present institutional configuration with marginal changes."[35] Rephrased, this argument holds that the systems model is biased toward the process of gradual or incremental change (or no change at all) because it interprets broader or more rapid change as a threat to the stability and even the continued existence of the system under study.

The fact that much political analysis has been biased toward the goal of stability cannot be refuted. Easton has himself concluded, "The equilibrium approach is seldom explicitly elaborated, yet it infuses a good part of political research, especially group politics and international relations . . . . A careful scrutiny of the language used reveals that equilibrium and stability are usually assumed to mean the same thing."[36] However, the systems model elaborated by Easton seeks to avoid this bias by focusing not on equilibrium but on "systems persistence." Easton's concept of "persistence" has been described by Morton Davies and Vaughan Lewis in this manner:

> Easton's system analysis is that analytical framework (or, for him, theory) which explains why a system is capable of persisting, not simply maintaining itself, but, if necessary, of adapting its structure to environmental stress. Persistence, according to his definition includes the idea that systems may change, and allows him to claim that his definition of a self-regulating political system implies a dynamic rather than a static analysis which he holds to be characteristic of the equilibrium approach.[37]

Thus Easton's systems model has no bias toward stability but rather seeks to explain how political systems adapt to changing conditions. One form of reaction is to change environmental conditions, but change in the political system itself is one of the most important means for adapting to stress. In Easton's words,

> For any social system, including the political, adaption represents more than simple adjustments to the events in its life, it is made up of efforts, limited only by the variety of human skills, resources, and ingenuity, to control, modify or *fundamentally change* either the environment or the *system itself* or both together.[38] (Emphasis added.)

In sum, we have reviewed three major criticisms of the behavioral approach—conservatism, fear of popular democracy, and avoidance of important issues—and found they do not apply to the systems model as it will be used in this study. While the model should be supplemented by a normative theory that can assign priority among research topics, it is nonetheless applicable to a wide variety of policy areas including antipoverty programs. While some behavioralists have not paid sufficient attention to mass movements in politics, the nature of the model does not preclude or hamper analysis of this form of participation. Finally, while there is a tendency among some researchers to equate equilibrium with stability, Easton's framework avoids this bias by focusing on "systems persistence," a concept that incorporates the necessity of change in the system itself as a response to stress.

NOTES

1. See his *A Framework for Political Analysis* (Englewood Cliffs, N.J.: Prentice-Hall, 1965) and his *A Systems Analysis of Political Life* (New York: John Wiley & Sons, 1965).

2. Robert Connery, *The Politics of Mental Health* (New York: Columbia University Press, 1968); John Donovan, *The Politics of Poverty* (New York: Pegasus, 1967); and Michael Armacost, *The Politics of Weapons Innovation* (New York: Columbia University Press, 1969).

3. Examples of the pluralist position are David Truman, *The Governmental Process* (New York: Alfred A. Knopf, 1960); and Robert Dahl, *Pluralist Democracy in the United States* (Chicago: Rand McNally, 1967).

4. On the positive side see James Wilson and Edward Banfield, "Public Regardingness as a Value Premise in Voting Behavior," *American Political Science Review (APSR)*, December 1964, pp. 876-87; and their *City Politics* (New York: Vintage, 1963). For differing views see Raymond Wolfinger and John Field, "Political Ethos and the Structure of City Government," in Terry Clark, ed., *Community Structure and Decision Making* (San Francisco: Chandler, 1968), pp. 159-95; Robert Lineberry and Edmund Fowler, "Reformism and Public Policies in American Cities," APSR, September 1967.

5. See Richard Dawson and James Robinson, "Inter-party Competition, Economic Variables, and Welfare Policies in the American States," *Journal of Politics* 21, pp. 265-89; and Thomas Dye, *Politics, Economics and the Public* (Chicago: Rand McNally, 1966).

6. Thomas Dye, "Income Inequality and American State Politics," *APSR*, March 1969, pp. 157-62.

7. Dye, *Politics, Economics and the Public*, p. 293.

8. Ira Sharkansky and Richard Hofferbert, "Dimensions of State Politics, Economics, and Public Policy," *APSR*, September 1969, p. 867. See also Hofferbert, "Socio-Economic Dimensions of American States, 1890-1960," *Midwest Journal of Politics*,

August 1968, pp. 401-18; and Charles Cnudde and Donald McCrone, "Party Competition and Welfare Policies in the American States," *APSR*, September 1969, pp. 858-66.

9. Sharkansky and Hofferbert, "Dimensions of State Politics," p. 867.

10. Harold Lasswell, *Politics: Who Gets What, When and How* (New York: McGraw-Hill, 1936).

11. Harold Lasswell, "The Policy Orientation," in Daniel Lerner and Harold Lasswell, eds., *The Policy Sciences* (Stanford, Cal.: Stanford University Press, 1960), pp. 3-15.

12. Ira Sharkansky, "Environment, Policy, Output, and Impact: Problems of Theory and Method in the Analysis of Public Policy," in Ira Sharkansky, ed., *Policy Analysis in Political Science* (Chicago: Markham, 1970), pp. 61-72.

13. Ira Sharkansky, "The Political Scientist and Policy Analysis," in Sharkansky, ed., *Policy Analysis in Political Science*, pp. 16-17.

14. Kenneth Dolbeare, "Public Policy Analysis and the Coming Struggle for the Soul of the Post-behavioral Revolution," in Philip Green and Sanford Levison, eds., *Power and Community* (New York: Vintage, 1970), p. 90.

15. Kenneth Dolbeare and James Davis, *Little Groups of Neighbors: The Selective Service System* (Chicago: Markham, 1968).

16. Kenneth Dolbeare and James Davis, "Selective Service and Military Manpower: Induction and Deferment Policies in the 1960's," in Austin Ranney, ed., *Political Science and Public Policy* (Chicago: Markham, 1968), pp. 83-121.

17. Donovan, *The Politics of Poverty*; and James Sundquist, *Politics and Policy: The Eisenhower, Kennedy and Johnson Years* (Washington, D.C.: The Brookings Institution, 1968).

18. Sar Levitan, *The Great Society's Poor Law: A New Approach to Poverty* (Baltimore: The Johns Hopkins Press, 1969); and Daniel Moynihan, *Maximum Feasible Misunderstanding: Community Action in the War on Poverty* (New York: The Free Press, 1969).

19. Peter Eisinger, "The Anti-Poverty Community Action Group as a Political Force in the Ghetto" (unpublished Ph.D. dissertation, Yale University, 1969).

20. Joseph Cepuran, "CAP Expenditures in the Fifty States: A Comparison," *Urban Affairs Quarterly*, March 1969, pp. 325-41.

21. David Greenstone and Paul Peterson, "Reformers, Machines and the War on Poverty," in James Wilson, ed., *City Politics and Public Policy* (New York: John Wiley & Sons, 1968), pp. 267-91.

22. Charles McCoy and John Playford, *Apolitical Politics: A Critique of Behavioralism* (New York: Thomas Y. Crowell, 1967), p. v.

23. *Ibid*, p. 3.

24. Christian Bay, "Politics and Pseudopolitics: A Critical Evaluation of Some Behavioral Literature," *APSR*, March 1965, p. 39.

25. Thomas Dye, *The Politics of Equality* (Indianapolis: Bodds-Merrill, 1971); and Bruce Russett, *What Price Vigilance?* (New Haven, Conn.: Yale University Press, 1970).

26. Bay, "Politics and Pseudopolitics," p. 40.

27. *Ibid.*, p. 50.

28. Jack Walker used the term "elitist theory of democracy" in his "A Critique of the Elitist Theory of Democracy," *APSR*, June 1966, pp. 285-95; Walker and Dahl agreed this phrase seemed inappropriate, in correspondence appearing in the same issue of the *APSR*; Peter Bachrach has revised the phrase in his *The Theory of Democratic Elitism: A Critique* (Boston: Little, Brown, 1967).

29. McCoy and Playford, *Apolitical Politics*, p. 6.

30. Bachrach, *Theory of Democratic Elitism*, pp. 86-87.

31. Walker, "Critique of the Elitist Theory of Democracy," p. 295.

32. Easton, *Systems Analysis of Political Life*, pp. 80-81.

33. *Ibid.*, p. 95.

34. *Ibid.*, pp. 88-89.

35. James Petras, "Ideology and United States Political Scientists," in McCoy and Playford, *Apolitical Politics*, pp. 76-77.

36. Easton, *Systems Analysis of Political Life*, p. 19.

37. Morton Davies and Vaughn Lewis, *Models of Political Systems* (New York: Praeger Publishers, 1971), pp. 50-51.

38. Easton, *Systems Analysis of Political Life*, p. 21.

CHAPTER
2

POVERTY AS
A POLICY PROBLEM

DEVELOPMENT OF THE POVERTY ISSUE

The 1960s was a decade in which domestic poverty was revived as an important intellectual and political concern in the United States. Early in the decade academics and elected officials recognized that the continued economic growth that they had long advocated would not eradicate poverty in America.

It is impossible to point with precision to the factors that drew the issue to the nation's attention. The presidential campaign of John F. Kennedy brought the candidate, the press, and thus the public, into contact with the poor of West Virginia. Theodore White's account of *The Making of the President, 1960* vividly describes Kennedy's shock in touring the impoverished state and notes, "Of all the emotional experiences of his preconvention campaign, Kennedy's exposure to the misery of the mining fields probably changed him most as a man."[1]

While a few scholars had studied income distribution in the United States in earlier years, Michael Harrington's brief and well-written book *The Other America,* which appeared in 1962, drew attention to those whom America's economic growth had left behind. He reminded those who had benefited from rising prosperity that "tens of millions of Americans are, at this very moment, maimed in body and spirit, existing at levels beneath those necessary for human decency."[2] A widely read *New Yorker Magazine* article by Dwight MacDonald further spread the word that nearly one of every four Americans was living in poverty.[3]

14

Poverty became an officially recognized problem in January 1964, when the president declared an "unconditional war" upon it in his State of Union message and the Council of Economic Advisors (CEA) devoted a portion of its annual report to the topic. The CEA clearly set forth the dimensions of the problem. Its 1964 report noted the decling rate at which poverty was being reduced in the United States and then concluded,

> The progress made since World War II has not involved any major changes in the distribution of incomes. The one-fifth of families with the highest incomes received an estimated 43 percent of total income in 1947 and 42 percent in 1963.
>   Even if poverty should hereafter decline at the relatively more rapid rate of the 1947-1956 period, there would still be 10 percent of the Nation's families in poverty in 1980. And, if the decline in poverty proceeded at the slower rate achieved from 1957 on, 13 percent of our families would still have incomes under $3,000 in 1980. We cannot leave the further wearing away of poverty solely to the general progress of the economy. A faster reduction of poverty will require that the lowest fifth of our families be able to earn a larger share of national output.[4]

Although by 1964 the goal of eliminating poverty had been adopted by the federal government and had achieved widespread popular support, there was no such unanimity regarding the policies or programs required to enable the bottom fifth of America's families to acquire a larger portion of the total national income. All that was agreed, as the CEA statement indicates, was that measures beyond continued economic growth were required to reduce poverty rapidly. With the benefit of hindsight we can identify two basic strategies that were advocated as a means for fighting poverty. We shall label them the "political strategy" and the "service strategy."

THE POLITICAL STRATEGY

The political strategy has as its basis the following set of assumptions: The distribution of income is determined primarily by the distribution of political power—that is to say, those with the most power get the most. Power is achieved and wielded through organization. For the poor to overcome their powerlessness they must become better organized. Therefore, the best antipoverty strategy is to encourage the development of organizations of the poor that will fight for their desired ends.

Perhaps the first contemporary advocate of the political strategy was the late Saul Alinsky. As early as 1946, Alinsky set forth a program aimed at enhancing the welfare of the poor through the formation of groups he called People's Organizations. He described his strategy as follows:

> The present power age defines and evaluates everything in terms of power. To this common and accepted view the field of organization has been no exception. It is universally assumed that the function of a People's Organization is similar to that of any other kind of organization, which is to become so strong, so powerful, that it can achieve its end.[5]

Several years later black leaders came to similar conclusions in analyzing the cause of continued poverty among American Negroes. Kenneth Clark's discussion of the problems of Harlem reflects an awareness of the need for ghetto residents to organize themselves in order to wield power. He began his chapter "Strategy for Change" in *Dark Ghetto* by saying:

> Stagnant ghettos are a monument to the dominance of forces which tend to perpetuate the *status quo* and to resist constructive social change. If the ghettos are to be transformed, then forces superior to those which resist change must be mobilized to counteract them. The problem of change in the ghetto is essentially, therefore, a problem of power—a confrontation and conflict between the power required for change and the power resistant to change . . . . The form of power that is most significant in the understanding of social change is that combination of energies required to determine and to translate goals into a desired social reality.[6]

The advocates of the political strategy who enjoyed the largest audience were Charles Hamilton and Stokely Carmichael. Their book set forth a political program, black power, which they described in the following manner: "It is a call for black people in this country to unite, to recognize their heritage, to build a sense of community. It is a call for black people to begin to define their own goals, to lead their own organizations and to support those organizations."[7]

In brief, a strategy first used by Alinsky in Chicago's mixed poverty areas was, in the 1960s, modified and adapted to the position of American blacks and advocated as a means for alleviating their poverty. This brief review is intended not as a definitive analysis and evaluation of the theory and its historical evolution but rather as a summary of the assumptions upon which it is based.

THE SERVICE STRATEGY

A second approach to the problem of increasing the proportion of income received by those in the lower fifth has its roots in the traditional social welfare services and more recent economic theory. The service strategy begins with the assumptions that (1) those in poverty differ in some way from the majority who are not so afflicted; (2) these differences stem from individual deficiencies and can be overcome through the provision of remedial services. Therefore, the best antipoverty strategy is to increase the services provided to the poor. The approach has been summarized by Moynihan:

> The conceptual issues on which an antipoverty program must be based comes to this: In which way are the poor different from others; how did they come to be that way; what measures could be expected to bring them into a sufficient measure of conformity with the needs of the larger society that they are no longer seen as poor and different; and no longer regard themselves as such?[8]

In a society in which employment is the most generally accepted means of livelihood, it is not surprising that adherents of the service strategy have noted that a significant way in which poor and nonpoor differ is their ability or willingness to secure employment. The more charitable members of this school of thought do not question the willingness of the poor to work but find them unable to get jobs because of the changing nature of the economy. Many of the poor are not supporting themselves through employment because they lack the skills required to secure steady employment in a technologically complex economy. "Structural unemployment," which economists define as unemployment caused by shifts in the occupational structure of the economy rather than variations in the business cycle, is viewed as a major source of poverty.[9]

The specific antipoverty strategy that results from this analysis is the expansion of education and training services for the poor. After being properly trained, the poor will have the skills required to compete successfully in the modern labor market and thus will become self-supporting.

Examples are again useful to illustrate the way in which this strategy has been applied to the issue of poverty as it emerged in the 1960s. An economist, August Bolino, writing on *Manpower and the City* introduces a key chapter by arguing,

The gist of Chapter 2 is that technological changes and changing consumer tastes are causing a twist in the demand for labor from the nontechnical to the technical. Technological progress, that is partly responsible for the record economic growth of the last eight years, has also helped to create two Americas. Great affluence coexists with abject poverty. Occupational shortages coexist with unemployment.

Unemployment means economic dependency, poor homes, poor neighborhoods and poor schools. Unemployment robs many of their manhood and helps to create man-less families and father-less homes. More employment opportunity is the only long-run solution. But additional employment opportunities can be purchased only with the coin of education or training. There is no easy way.[10]

The Kerner Commission provided a similar analysis and recommendations. It found that "the most compelling and difficult challenge is presented by some 500,000 'hardcore' who live within the central cities, lack a basic education, work not at all or only from time to time and are unable to cope with the problems of holding and performing a job."[11] Among their many recommendations was one for "concentrated job training efforts with major emphasis on on-the-job training by both public and private employers, as well as public and private vocational school and other institutional facilities."[12]

The Committee for Economic Development, a prestigious national organization of business executives and academics, has issued similar analyses and recommendations. In September 1965, it published a report recommending *Raising Low Income Through Improved Education*,[13] and in 1970 its study of *Training and Jobs for the Urban Poor* urged expansion of federal, state, and local efforts in job training.[14]

Two other approaches to the problem of poverty should also be noted. One is simply reliance on economic growth and the maintenance of "full employment," a term economists use to refer to an unemployment rate of between 3 and 4 percent. This approach is not considered here because it is generally agreed that this policy alone is not an effective antipoverty program. As the passage quoted from the CEA revealed, recent history has shown that in the United States economic growth alone will not serve to redistribute income quickly. Hence, we are concerned with those policies besides economic growth that are necessary to reduce poverty.

The second approach has been referred to as the "income strategy." This refers to expansion of income transfer programs rather than new service programs to provide higher incomes to the poor. Specific proposals range from the Nixon Administration's Family Assistance Program to the recommendation of the Heineman Commission to revise the present welfare system to create "a universal income supplement program financed by the federal government, making cash payments to all members of the population with income needs,"[15] and to the more drastic proposals for children's allowances[16] or a negative income tax.[17] However, these proposals share a common feature that disqualifies them from consideration in this study—they remain in the proposal stage and have not been adopted as public policy. This fact points up one of the flaws of the income strategy: Advocates have been unable to specify a method for gaining the popular and congressional support necessary to enact a significantly revised income transfer system.[18]

POVERTY—DEFINITION AND TRENDS

Poverty may be defined as an absolute or as a relative concept. Lester Thurow has set forth four bases for defining poverty, two of which use absolute criteria and two of which use relative criteria.[19] Absolute definitions of poverty include (1) estimates of the income necessary to guarantee survival and (2) estimates of the income needed to yield an adequate standard of living as seen by the majority of the population. The minimal survival definition is most appropriate to underdeveloped countries and is rarely used in the United states. It covers only the income necessary to purchase food embodying the minimum number of calories necessary for human life to continue. Even our "poor" are expected to do more than merely survive and to consume more than the basic diet required for subsistence. Official definitions usually employ the minimum-adequate-standard-of-living approach. Individuals or agencies may differ over what is "adequate." The CEA in its 1964 report arbitrarily drew the poverty line at $3,000 per family per year. In the same year the Social Security Administration calculated it to be $3,128 for a family of four.[20] This was arrived at by specifying a "bundle of goods" that a family would have to purchase during a year in order to maintain a minimally adequate standard of living. The items included in this package have not been changed since 1964, but because of general price increases (inflation), an income of $3,968 was required to purchase these goods in 1970. Thus, inflation has driven the official poverty line up, but this represents no increase in the standard of living provided by a poverty income.

Relative approaches define poverty as either (3) a fraction of the income distribution or (4) deviations from explicit goals for the shape of the income distribution. Under the third definition the poor are simply those in the bottom 10 percent (or 5 percent or 20 percent) of the income distribution. This definition of poverty is basically descriptive, and poverty, so defined, can never be eliminated. However, one can use this approach to judge the equity of the income distribution as measured by the share of total income received by those families at the lowest end of the income distribution.

In the last and most sophisticated definition, poverty is defined in relation to a desired shape of the national income distribution. For example, poverty lines may be drawn at 50 percent of median family income with the implicit notion that the desired shape for the income distribution is one in which no family receives less than half the median income for all families. Poverty is eliminated when no individual or family has an income less than half the median income for all individuals or families. The exact amount required will rise or fall with the general level of prosperity.

The implications of the alternative poverty definitions become clear when we examine the actual income distribution figures for the United States for the period 1947-71 (See Table 2.1). The first two columns in Table 2.1 show the relative stability of the over-all income distribution. While the share of total income received by families in the bottom one-fifth of the income distribution rose steadily, but slightly, between 1961 and 1968, it decreased since 1968 to 5.5 percent in 1970 and 1971. The share received by the top one-fifth has fluctuated slightly in recent years, with lows of 40.5 percent in 1957 and 40.6 percent in 1968 and rising to 41.6 percent in 1970 and 1971.

The third column in Table 2.1 shows trends in poverty based on a minimum-adequate-level definition. Because of changes in the consumer price index, the standard package of goods specified by the Social Security Administration represents an income for a family of four of $4,137 in 1971; $3,968 in 1970; $3,743 in 1969; $3,553 in 1968; $3,169 in 1964; and $2,973 in 1959.[21] Using this definition, the trend is a reduction in poverty from 22.4 percent in 1959 to 12.2 percent in 1969 with a rise in 1970 to 12.6 percent (the years in Table 2.1 are the only ones for which detailed figures including family size are available).

Trends in poverty based on a relative income definition, rather than a fixed minimum standard, can be derived from the last column in Table 2.1, which shows the national median income. The median family income rose from $3,031 in 1947 to $10,285 in 1971. If a relative poverty line is drawn at half the median, then the poverty line would have risen from $1,515 in 1947 to $5,143 in 1971. Below are the poverty lines for the years for which data are available using both the relative definition (half the median) and the absolute or fixed package of goods definition:

Year	Relative	Absolute
1959	$2,708	$2,973
1964	3,285	3,169
1968	4,316	3,553
1969	4,716	3,743
1970	4,933	3,968
1971	5,143	4,137

TABLE 2.1

Income Distribution in United States, 1947-71

Year	Percent of All Income Received by		Percent of All Families Below Official Poverty Line	Median Income of All Families
	Top Fifth	Bottom Fifth		
1947	43.0	5.0	-	$ 3,031
1950	42.6	4.3	-	3,319
1957	40.5	5.0	-	-
1958	40.9	5.1	-	5,087
1959	41.4	5.0	22.4	5,417
1960	42.0	4.9	-	5,620
1961	42.6	4.8	-	5,737
1962	41.7	5.1	-	5,956
1963	41.4	5.1	-	6,249
1964	41.1	5.2	19.0	6,569
1965	41.3	5.3	-	6,957
1966	40.7	5.5	-	7,500
1967	41.2	5.4	-	7,974
1968	40.6	5.7	12.8	8,632
1969	41.0	5.6	12.2	9,433
1970	41.6	5.5	12.6	9,867
1971	41.6	5.5	12.5	10,285

Source: Current Population Reports, U.S. Bureau of the Census, Series P-60, No. 85, "Money Income in 1971 of Families and Persons in the United States" (Washington, D.C., 1972), Tables 8 and 14; *Current Population Reports,* U.S. Bureau of the Census, Series P-60, No. 86, "Characteristics of the Low Income Population, 1971" (Washington, D.C., 1972), Table A.

063526

Data are not available to compute the precise percentage of people in poverty based on the relative definition. However, some general idea of the trend can be gained by comparing the percentage of families with the incomes under $3,000 in 1959 (when the relative line was $2,708) to the percentage under $5,000 in 1970 (when the relative line was $4,933). These figures are 31.5 percent and 29.7 percent, respectively.[22] Thus, using a relative definition of poverty we find the problem is more extensive and has diminished significantly less over time than when we use an absolute definition.

CHARACTERISTICS OF THE POOR AND THE INCIDENCE OF POVERTY

It is helpful to gain some familiarity with the characteristics of the poor population before evaluating strategies to alleviate poverty. Data on this topic are presented in Table 2.2. The figures refer to families below the official federal (fixed minimum standard) definition of poverty in 1971. This is the only group for which comprehensive data are available.

The first two columns in Table 2.2 show the distribution of all families in the United States, and the second two columns give the distribution of poor families. Examining the characteristics of the poor population we see that of the total number of poor families (5,303,000) approximately 71 percent are white and 60 percent are headed by males. About 34 percent of the poor families reside in central cities, 22 percent in the suburbs and nearly half (44 percent) in nonmetropolitan areas. About 20 percent of the poor families are headed by elderly persons. Approximately 53 percent of the poor families are headed by a person who has some civilian employment, and the bulk of this group work full-time; about 46 percent of the poor families had a head who did not work.

As important as the characteristics of the poor is the incidence of poverty. This refers to the percentage of a specified group within the population who are poor and indicates those groups for whom poverty is a particularly acute problem. The last column in Table 2.2 reports the incidence of poverty among selected groups. Over-all, about 10 percent of all American families have incomes below the federal poverty line. However, one-third (34 percent) of all female-headed families and over one-quarter (27 percent) of all nonwhite families are poor. About 30 percent of all families without a working head are poor, and for those working part-time the figure is 23 percent. The incidence of poverty is higher among nonmetropolitan families (14 percent) than among those in central cities (11 percent) and is lowest among suburban families.

We may summarize by stating that under the federal definition of poverty the majority of poor families are headed by white males in their prime years who are working. However, poverty is most prevalent, and is

TABLE 2.2

Characteristics of All Families and of Poor
Families in United States, 1971

(numbers in thousands)

	All Families		Poor Families		Incidence of Poverty
	Number	Percent	Number	Percent	
Total	53,296	100.0	5,303	100.0	10.0
Sex of head					
Male	47,105	88.4	3,203	60.4	6.8
Female	6,191	11.6	2,100	39.6	33.9
Race of head					
White	47,641	89.4	3,751	70.7	7.9
Nonwhite	5,655	10.6	1,552	29.3	27.4
Work experience of head					
In armed forces	1,020	1.9	72	1.4	7.1
Did not work	8,108	15.2	2,422	45.7	29.9
Worked full-time	41,055	77.0	2,082	39.3	5.1
Worked part-time	3,133	5.9	727	13.7	23.4
Residence					
Central city	16,114	30.2	1,781	33.6	11.1
Suburb	20,382	38.2	1,189	22.4	5.8
Nonmetropolitan	16,800	31.5	2,333	44.0	13.9
Age of head					
Under 25	3,993	7.5	719	13.6	18.0
25-64 yrs.	41,816	78.5	3,522	66.4	8.4
65 and over	7,487	14.0	1,062	20.0	14.2

Source: Current Population Reports, U.S. Bureau of the Census, Series P-60, No. 86, "Characteristics of the Low Income Population, 1971" (Washington, D.C., 1972).

consequently an even more serious problem, among black- and female-headed families, and for older and rural families, many of who are not working and are incapable of working in the future.

NOTES

1. Theodore White, *The Making of the President, 1960* (New York: Atheneum, 1961), p. 106.

2. Michael Harrington, *The Other America* (Baltimore: Penguin Books, 1963), p. 9.

3. Dwight MacDonald, "Our Invisible Poor," The *New Yorker,* January 19, 1963, pp. 82-92.

4. *Economic Report of the President,* transmitted to the Congress in January 1964, together with the *Annual Report* of the Council of Economic Advisors (Washington, D.C., 1964), pp. 60-61.

5. Saul Alinsky, *Reveille for Radicals* (New York: Vintage 1969), p. 53.

6. Kenneth Clark, *Dark Ghetto* (New York: Harper & Row, 1965), p. 199.

7. Stokely Carmichael and Charles Hamilton, *Black Power* (New York: Vintage, 1967), p. 44.

8. D. Moynihan, "The Professors and the Poor," in Daniel Moynihan, ed., *On Understanding Poverty: Perspectives from the Social Sciences* (New York: Basic Books, 1969), p. 21.

9. See any introductory economics text, for example Campbell McConnell, *Economics* (New York: McGraw-Hill, 1966), pp. 374-78.

10. August Bolino, *Manpower and the City* (Cambridge, Mass.: Shenkman, 1969), p. 37.

11. *Report,* National Advisory Commission on Civil Disorders (New York: Bantam Books, 1968), p. 515.

12. *Ibid.,* p. 415.

13. Committee for Economic Development, *Raising Low Income Through Improved Education* (New York: the Committee, 1965).

14. Committee for Economic Development, *Training and Jobs for the Urban Poor* (New York: the Committee, 1970).

15. *Poverty amid Plenty: The American Paradox,* President's Commission on Income Maintenance Programs (Washington, D.C., 1969), p. 7.

16. See for example Eveline Burns, ed., *Children's Allowances and the Economic Welfare of Children* (New York: Citizens' Committee for Children, 1968).

17. Criteria for comparing the various proposals are suggested in Theodore Marmor, "On Comparing Income Maintenance Alternatives," *American Political Science Review*, March 1971, pp. 83-96.

18. A discussion of the problem appears in Gilbert Steiner, *The State of Welfare* (Washington, D.C.: The Brookings Institution, 1971), pp. 320-37.

19. Lester Thurow, *Poverty and Discrimination* (Washington, D.C.: The Brookings Institution, 1969), pp. 20-21.

20. See Mollie Orshansky, "Counting the Poor: Another Look at the Poverty Profile," *Social Security Bulletin*, January 1965, pp. 2-29.

21. *Current Population Reports*, U.S. Bureau of Census, Series P-60, No. 86, "Characteristics of the Low Income Population, 1971" (Washington, D.C., 1972), Table L, p. 17.

22. Calculations based on data from *Current Population Reports*, U.S. Bureau of Census, "Income in 1970 of Families and Persons in the United States" (Washington, D.C., 1971), Table 8, p. 22.

3

FEDERAL ANTIPOVERTY
PROGRAMS AND STRATEGIES

This chapter will describe the legislative development of two programs identified with the federal antipoverty effort—the Manpower Development and Training Act of 1962 (MDTA) and the Economic Opportunity Act of 1964 (EOA). In each case we shall examine the origins and provisions of the statute and relate them to the strategies outlined earlier. It will be argued that the MDTA may clearly be identified with the service strategy, that the EOA includes a mixture of approaches, but the Title II community action programs represent an opportunity to create programs committed to the political strategy.

THE MANPOWER DEVELOPMENT AND TRAINING ACT

The MDTA has its origins in the economic conditions and theories that prevailed in the last half of the 1950s and the early 1960s.[1] After the Korean War, unemployment rose and remained above 4 percent until 1958, when it reached almost 7 percent. Throughout the period the rate for blacks remained substantially higher than that for whites (See Table 3.1). During this period, senators from industrial states whose constituents were affected by the growing unemployment introduced bills to encourage job growth in their areas. A bill was introduced in 1955 by Senator Paul Douglas (D.-Ill.), Senator John F. Kennedy (D.-Mass.), and six other Democratic cosponsors that provided for special loans to firms locating in regions defined as distressed areas. The legislation encountered considerable opposition and was

TABLE 3.1

Average Annual Unemployment Rates, 1947-71

Year	Total	Black	White
1947	3.9	*	*
1948	3.8	5.9	3.5
1949	5.9	8.9	5.6
1950	5.3	9.0	4.9
1951	3.3	5.3	3.1
1952	3.0	5.4	2.8
1953	2.9	4.5	2.7
1954	5.5	9.9	5.0
1955	4.4	8.7	3.9
1956	4.1	8.3	3.6
1957	4.3	7.9	3.8
1958	6.8	12.6	6.1
1959	5.5	10.7	4.8
1960	5.5	10.2	4.9
1961	6.7	12.4	6.0
1962	5.5	10.9	4.9
1963	5.7	10.8	5.0
1964	5.2	9.6	4.6
1965	4.5	8.1	4.1
1966	3.8	7.3	3.3
1967	3.8	7.4	3.4
1968	3.6	6.7	3.2
1969	3.5	6.4	3.1
1970	4.9	8.2	4.5
1971	5.9	9.9	5.4

*Separate figures by race not available for 1947.

Source: Manpower Report of the President, U.S. Department of Labor, March 1972 (Washington, D.C., 1972), Table A-14, p. 175.

modified and reintroduced several times. In 1958 it was passed by both the House and Senate. However, President Dwight D. Eisenhower vetoed it, objecting to specific provisions regarding the loan terms and the more general trend toward federal action that might absolve state and local officials of responsibility for assisting depressed areas.

Unemployment was a central theme of the 1958 elections, and the results were a sweeping victory for the Democrats. In 12 Senate seats and 49 House seats Democrats replaced Republicans. In the early spring of 1959 the AFL-CIO organized a march on Washington to demand action. The Senate majority leader, Lyndon Baines Johnson, responded by proposing a special commission consisting of three senators, three House members, and five presidential appointees that would be responsible for making recommendations within 60 days. The resolution passed the Senate (on April 8, 1959) and was endorsed by the President (on April 14, 1959) but for unknown reasons never got past the desk of House Speaker Sam Rayburn.[2]

Finally, on September 12, 1959, the Senate created its own Special Committee on Unemployment to examine the problem and make appropriate recommendations. It is one of history's ironies that in appointing the committee's chairman, Majority Leader Johnson passed over several senior senators who had been identified with the issue and awarded the position to freshman Senator Eugene McCarthy of Minnesota. The committee did an admirable job. Its nine volumes of testimony take in 12 states; 1,700 pages of selected readings and 15 special studies are considered a classic reference for those interested in the problems of unemployment.[3] The committee's efforts emphasized the need for structural measures to deal with unemployment and poverty. Its report, issued in March 1960, gave highest priority to passage of the depressed area program Democrats had supported since 1955, but it also urged creation of a nation-wide vocational education program supported by federal grants to help unemployed workers train for new jobs. Specifically, with respect to training, the special committee's report stated,

> The committee recommends cooperation by all levels of government to provide greatly expanded facilities for preparing young people to enter the employment market and for assisting older workers whose skills have become unmarketable to obtain retraining. The committee recommends institution of a nation-wide vocational training program through Federal grants-in-aid to the states including specialized courses for youth who have dropped out of school and for older workers who require retraining.[4]

The committee's recommendations and the presidential election of 1960 produced several pieces of proposed legislation. Senator Douglas again sought passage of his area redevelopment bill, Senator Joseph S. Clark (D.-Pa.) introduced a public works bill and also had William Cooper, the head of Pennsylvania's vocational education services, draft a bill for federal support of vocational training for adults. As a favor to Senator Jennings Randolph of West Virginia, who was fighting a close battle for reelection, Clark let Randolph introduce the training bill. Randolph was also made chairman of the newly created Subcommittee on Employment and Manpower of the Senate Labor and Public Welfare Committee with the understanding that Clark would take over the position after Randolph's reelection.

No new manpower legislation was enacted in 1960, but a new president, committed to reducing unemployment and, in fact, committed to each of the bills, all of which had been incorporated in the Democratic platform, was elected. In 1961 the new administration and Congress acted quickly and the first major piece of legislation produced by the Kennedy Administration was Senator Douglas's Area Redevelopment Act. (The number of the bill was S.1.)

Clark's vocational education bill, which did not have six years of hearings and review behind it, was not so quickly enacted. Not that many questioned the efficacy of training adults. Economists fought over the relative significance of structural factors as opposed to aggregate demand in causing unemployment,[5] but this did not endanger the bill. Both schools of thought favored training, the question was whether it should be a supplement to or a substitute for fiscal measures (that is, tax cut or increased government expenditures).

The issue that blocked passage of the training bill in 1961 was who should be responsible for administering the training program. Clark's original proposal, drafted by the head of Pennsylvania's vocational education services, provided that grants be given to public high schools in a manner similar to the way vocational education grants for high-school-age students had been dispersed under the Smith-Hughes Act dating back to 1917. The Department of Health, Education, and Welfare (HEW), which administered the Smith-Hughes program and dispersed the funds on a formula basis to state boards of education, favored this approach, as did the American Vocational Association (AVA), the interest group representing the vocational educators.

However, vocational education as practiced in the high schools was generally recognized as a second-class effort. Officials in the Bureau of the Budget (BOB) and the Department of Labor (DOL) wanted something better. The administration bill introduced in 1961 placed control of the program under the Secretary of Labor, not HEW, and permitted him to negotiate training arrangements with a variety of agencies rather than an automatic distribution of funds to the states. The AVA strongly opposed the bill, arguing that established institutions were best equipped to do the training job. The nature of the opposition is well expressed in the testimony of AVA President William B. Logan before the Senate Subcommittee on Employment and Manpower:

> No one will dispute the fact that there is a great need for training
> and retraining the people who have been displaced by automation

or other technological developments, foreign competition, relocation of industry, shifts in market demand, or other changes in the structure of the economy . . . . The question we raise is, who can do the job of training most efficiently and effectively to get the unemployed back into production.[6]

Logan supplied the answer to his question:

> Every State and Territory has a state board for vocational education that has full authority to administer Federal vocational funds. These boards have had more than 40 years of successful experience in developing and administering vocational education programs. The programs under their direction are so organized that they can be revamped and adjusted almost overnight to meet changing conditions.[7]

The Senate committee substantially amended the bill to meet the AVA's demands. The committee's bill, which converted the program to an HEW-funded and state-administered vocational education effort, was passed by the Senate. However, the House Education and Labor Committee did not similarly revise the administration's bill before passing it. As a result, the AVA successfully lobbied to prevent the House bill from emerging from the House Rules Committee in 1961.

In 1962 the Manpower Development and Training Act passed in a form acceptable to HEW, the DOL, and the AVA. The law provided for two different types of training—institutional and on the job (OJT); there is also a provision for experimental and demonstration projects. The institutional training program was jointly administered by DOL and HEW. It provided for classroom training under the sponsorship of state vocational education agencies. HEW was responsible for distributing funds to the states to establish these programs. The DOL had to certify that the proposed training was appropriate and that a local labor market need existed for such workers. The DOL also was responsible for dispensing allowances to eligible trainees. To be eligible a trainee had to be a head of a household who was unemployed but had at least three years' prior work experience. Allowances were equal to the maximum unemployment insurance payments provided by the state.

In practice, a typical institutional program worked as follows: A local school district proposes to its state education department the creation of a training course for adults for a specific occupation. If the state education department approves, and the U.S. Department of Labor approves the program, the Department of Health, Education, and Welfare may then enter into a contract with the school for the cost of the program. Enrollees are referred by the local employment service. Enrollees meeting the eligibility criteria described above are paid a weekly allowance by the employment service.

After completing the course the trainee is assisted by the employment service in finding a job in his new occupation.

The OJT program was under the exclusive jurisdiction of the Secretary of Labor. He entered into contracts with employers to provide training for workers. The government contracts with the employer to cover the added supervisory, wastage, and other training-related costs. Employers were obliged to pay the trainees at least the minimum wage.

In practice, the OJT program worked as follows: The DOL would contract with a trade association or similar organization for a fixed amount of money as payment for training a specified number of workers in an occupation found in that industry. The associations would then subcontract to individual employers who actually recruited the trainees and performed the training. Alternatively, the DOL could negotiate a contract directly with a large employer.

The creation of two training programs, institutional and on the job, and the division of administrative responsibility between HEW and DOL represented a compromise over the basic issue preventing passage, that is, the question of bureaucratic control. Once this issue was resolved there was little opposition to the bill. The MDTA passed both houses with wide margins— 354 to 62 in the House and 60 to 31 in the Senate.

As passed in 1962, the MDTA could not be identified as an antipoverty program. Its primary aim was not to help those raised in poverty, but rather to help those who in the past had earned a living for themselves and their families (specifically, individuals who were heads of households with three years' previous work experience). The model trainee was a displaced coal miner from Senator Clark's Pennsylvania who had never before been poor and who would now be trained for a more technically complex job.

However, there was an early understanding among drafters of the bill that the program would give special attention to disadvantaged blacks. While it never became part of the official record, several congressional leaders had agreed that the program could be of special benefit to blacks. This point was made by Lyndon Johnson at the first meeting of the National Manpower Advisory Committee, a group of academic, labor, and business leaders appointed by the president to advise on the program's administration. The committee chairman's letter to the Secretary of Labor reporting the recommendations of that meeting contained the following paragraph:

We noted that the Department of Labor would have to take special effort to see to it that States in which discrimination is rife allocate their funds in such a manner that members of minority groups have an opportunity to benefit from training. The importance of such action is the greater because of what the Vice President related to us about the legislative history of the act. Many of its supporters recognized the need to help unskilled Negroes to become self-supporting.[8]

This early concern for disadvantaged blacks and a revival in the economy that began to reduce unemployment rates led to amendments to the MDTA enacted between 1963 and 1966 that transformed the program into an example of the service strategy. Soon after the legislation became operational, officials realized that the number of "trainable" trainees, and especially those who met the qualifications for allowances, was not as large as expected. Only one year after the program went into effect Labor Secretary W. Willard Wirtz testified before Congress that reaching the "hardcore" of poorly educated workers with limited histories of work experience was one of the biggest problems in administering MDTA. He pointed out that 20 percent of all the unemployed had less than an eighth grade education, but only 3 percent of MDTA trainees were drawn from this group. Almost 45 percent of the nation's unemployed black workers had less than an eighth grade education, but only 5 percent of the black MDTA trainees were from this group.[9]

In 1963 Congress passed amendments providing trainee allowances and institutional grants for up to 20 weeks of basic education prior to entering specific occupational training. In addition members of households who were not themselves heads of households, but whose heads were unemployed, were made eligible for allowances. The allowances were also raised $10. The requirement of three years' work experience was dropped to two years. Further liberalization in 1965 added up to $20 to the allowances of those with multiple dependents and permitted allowances to be paid single persons living alone.

Administrative changes and legislative developments in 1966 further reoriented the program to an antipoverty effort. By early 1966 the national unemployment rate had dropped below 4 percent, yet the nation was beginning to experience disruptive racial unrest. In the 1966 *Manpower Report of the President,* the Secretary of Labor noted that "certain groups in the Nation have not shared fully in the benefits of our unprecedented economic expansion. Much remains to be done to achieve full opportunity for these groups."[10] In fact, in 1966 the unemployment rate for blacks was 7.3 percent, well over double that of whites (3.3 percent).

One of the major tools in the DOL's effort to expand employment opportunities for the disadvantaged was training under the MDTA. The Secretary of Labor provided in 1966 that 65 percent of all training under the act would be reserved for the disadvantaged. Rather than helping those temporarily unemployed, the MDTA was henceforth to assist those who had never been able to support themselves successfully. The disadvantaged were to be given skills that would enable them to increase their earnings.

A further revision strengthening MDTA's antipoverty orientation took place in 1968. In his State of the Union Message, President Johnson stated, "This year, the time has come when we must get to those who are last in line—the hard-core unemployed—the hardest to reach," and he promised "to start a new partnership between government and private industry to train and to hire the hard-core unemployed persons."[11] Johnson kept his promise by submitting a Special Message to Congress on January 23, 1968, that proposed a revised manpower program: "To press the attack on the problem of the jobless in our cities, I propose that we launch the Job Opportunities in the Business Sector (JOBS) program—a new partnership between government and private industry to train and hire the hard-core unemployed."[12]

The new JOBS program resembled OJT under MDTA except that it was explicitly and exclusively designed to help the urban disadvantaged. Instead of contracting with various trade associations and other groups or with individual employers, the DOL worked with the newly formed National Alliance of Businessmen (NAB), which contracted with local Alliances and individual employers, for on-the-job training. Regulations governing reimbursable costs were liberalized, and employers could receive up to $3,500 per trainee. However, unlike the MDTA OJT program, trainees had to be certified as disadvantaged by the state employment service. Funds for the new program were drawn from existing appropriations for MDTA and selected OEO programs. The MDTA OJT program was phased out beginning in 1970 and has been replaced by the JOBS and related programs.

In summary, since its enactment in 1962, the MDTA has been transformed through amendment and administrative reform into a program whose primary aim is to assist the poor by increasing their earnings through occupational training.

THE ECONOMIC OPPORTUNITY ACT OF 1964

Chapter 2 indicated that in the early 1960s poverty became an issue that attracted considerable public attention. However, there elapsed some time before the concern was transformed into legislation. The precise beginnings of the process remain shrouded.[13] Sar Levitan credits the initiative to Robert Lampman, a staff economist with the Council of Economic Advisors. He writes, "Every good story must have its hero, and it was Lampman who performed the role of catalyst in bringing poverty to the attention of the highest government level."[14] According to Levitan's version Lampman, who had a long-standing interest in the problems of low-income families, began discussing the subject with CEA Chairman Walter Heller. Heller proved to be sympathetic and took initiatives to develop a program in early 1963, presumably after receiving presidential approval in principle.

James Sundquist's version of the program's conception is slightly different.[15] He reports that Kennedy had a year-end review of the economic status of the nations with Heller in December of 1962 and at that time urged the chairman to look for new issues and specifically asked about the poverty problem. Heller then assigned Lampman to assemble data on the topic.

Regardless of who the "true hero" is, it is apparent that in early 1963 Heller and Lampman began working on the issue. Lampman prepared a staff paper in May and by August had completed a draft for a chapter on poverty for the January 1964 *Economic Report of the President.* Meanwhile, Heller issued a trail balloon and made reference to the need to combat poverty in the U.S. in a speech to the Communications Workers of America in June. During the summer Heller assembled an informal group consisting of four of his staff workers, three BOB officials, and two White House aides. They considered the advisability of developing the "poverty issue" in the forthcoming election year (1964) and weighed possible approaches.

President Kennedy's attitude toward the proposals seems to have been favorable. His aides Arthur Schlesinger, Jr., and Theodore Sorenson have separately written that the president gave Heller's group encouragement to develop proposals for the 1964 legislative program of the administration some time in October 1963.[16] On November 5, Heller circulated a memorandum to each of the major departments requesting suggestions for possible inclusion in the 1964 legislative program. On November 19, the president gave Heller a definite affirmative answer to Heller's blunt question about whether or not his legislative package would include antipoverty measures.

On November 22, 1963, President Kennedy was shot and killed in Dallas. Heller's first meeting with President Johnson took place on November 23, and Johson gave Heller a firm commitment. According to Heller he said, "That is my kind of program. It will help people. I want you to move full speed ahead on it."[17]

With a firm presidential commitment, a CEA-BOB group was assigned the task of formulating a concrete legislative proposal. Heller's memorandum of November 5 had yielded a long list of proposals from each agency, many of which were actually bills that had been drafted or submitted in earlier years, but that had not been passed. Among the proposals was one by David Hackett of the President's Committee on Juvenile Delinquency (PCJD) to create community organizations similar to those the committee and the Ford Foundation's Public Affairs Department had been funding in several cities. Hackett and Richard Boone of the foundation later met with Heller and an aide who, in turn, discussed the idea with the entire group. BOB officials liked the proposal and suggested creating 10 such community-based organizations as demonstration projects.

Meanwhile, decisions had to be made on the amount of funds for the program so it could be given a line in the annual budget, which had to be submitted in January. The BOB set a figure of $500 million in "new" funds and $500 million to be allocated from programs already in existence. This was to finance the "unconditional war on poverty" that the president declared in his State of the Union Message:

Unfortunately, many Americans live on the outskirts of hope, some because of their poverty and some because of their color, and all too many because of both. Our task is to help replace this despair with opportunity. And this Administration today, here and now, declares unconditional war on poverty in America, and I urge this Congress and all Americans to join with me in that effort.[18]

While the CEA-BOB group had reached tentative agreement on the nature of the program—community organizations similar to those created by the PCJD—there was still considerable debate over how it would be administered. The logical candidate was HEW; it controlled the juvenile delinquency program and was responsible for welfare and related programs designed to aid the poor. However the community action concept, as we shall note later, was still not precisely defined. It had connotations of coordination and over-all planning, powers that no department wanted to grant to a rival cabinet agency. The idea of an independent agency reporting directly to the president was suggested, and Johnson appeared to like it. With this in mind he appointed R. Sargent Shriver to head a new committee whose assignment was to review the proposals and formulate a bill.

Shriver, appointed on February 1, 1964, had been head of the Peace Corps and had not participated in the work completed up to then on the poverty program. Shriver assembled a task force. The new task force consulted over 130 different individuals including the CEA-BOB group and Ford Foundation officials. Shriver retained the community action concept but yielded to other departmental interests and added other projects. The bill drafted by Shriver's task force and submitted to Congress on March 16, 1964, contained six titles and authorized expenditures totaling $967.5 million. Title II, the Community Action Program (CAP), accounted for $315 million, or about one-third of the total. The remainder was divided among five other titles containing programs advocated by various departments.

Title I mandated a Neighborhood Youth Corps to provide jobs for teenagers and a Job Corps program of residential centers for youth based on the Youth Conservation Corps bill, which had been submitted in previous years by the Department of Labor. The Neighborhood Youth Corps was to be administered by the DOL while the Job Corps, along with the CAP, was to be administered by an independent Office of Economic Opportunity (OEO), which the bill created. Title III established a rural assistance program providing low-cost loans to farmers and rural businessmen, which was to be administered by the Department of Agriculture. Title IV contained a special loan program for low-income businessmen, which had been advocated by the Small Business Administration. Title V provided a special job program for welfare recipients. This program, to be administered by HEW, was almost identical to one that was authorized in the Public Welfare Amendments of 1962 but that had not been widely accepted because it required substantial financial participation by state and local governments rather than the almost total (90 percent) federal funding provided in the new bill. Finally, Title VI contained a Volunteers for America (later Volunteers in Service to America, or VISTA) program that resembled the Peace Corps and was similar to the National Service Corps bill, which passed the Senate in 1963. In brief, Shriver's group retained the Community Action Program advocated by the Ford Foundation and the PCJD but added to it several programs supported by competing cabinet departments.

Congress acted in just five months and passed the bill with only a few minor modifications. The Job Corps program was required by Congress to have 40 percent of its enrollees engaged in conservation work and females were made eligible for the program. An adult basic education bill that had been submitted to Congress several years earlier was added by the House and incorporated into the legislation. Other minor amendments in several titles were passed, but none substantially altered the bill. In August the bill secured final congressional approval, and it was signed into law on August 20, 1964.

The legislative history of the EOA provides an excellent example of the trend toward greater involvement by the executive branch in the legislative process. This trend was noted as early as 1942 by Edwin Wittle, who wrote, "In this recent period a very large percentage of all public bills acted on in Congress have originated in the administrative agencies of the government."[19] The EOA is a recent example of the dominant role played by the executive branch in producing public policy. As John Bibby and Roger Davidson have noted in their case study of the EOA,

> The most significant feature of the Economic Opportunity Act, from our point of view, was that it was "legislated" almost entirely within the executive branch and, indeed, virtually without prodding from Congressional or other "outside" clienteles .... Ill-prepared Congressmen opened hearings a day after the bill was sent to Capitol Hill; and the Congressional amendments were, at most, marginal to the substance of the legislation.[20]

Because the EOA was "legislated" almost entirely by the executive branch, we should focus on that part of its history in order to determine the extent to which it conforms to the political stragegy. Although congressmen and congressional committees are the official authors of the legislation, congressional hearings provide little insight into the nature of the CAP.

As submitted to Congress by the executive branch, the EOA represented an amalgam of programs advocated by various federal agencies. Of the admixture, only the CAP (Title II) can be identified with what we earlier described as the political strategy. In addition it is not certain that even this program was intended to carry out the political approach exclusively. The CAP provisions were based upon the experience of similar programs funded by the Ford Foundation and the PCJD. A careful study of these activities by Peter Marris and Martin Rein has concluded that the sponsors themselves had not clearly identified their strategy.[21] The authors argue that the agencies vacillated between three possible approaches. One, planning, is identified with social science research and the thoughtful development of theories and programs to be tested and accompanied in execution by extensive data collection. The second is a coalition among the numerous distinct and often isolated existing social service agencies to foster greater effectiveness in their endeavors. The third closely resembles what we have called the political strategy and calls for advocacy on behalf of the poor for the causes they support. When the community action approach was first recommended to the CEA-BOB group drafting the bill, it was not perceived as consisting solely of any one of these three approaches.

We can only speculate as to what the drafters and Congress had in mind when they embraced the community action approach. It is reasonable to assume that the Shriver group was not considering the careful planning approach. Shriver explicitly excluded preliminary planning or a demonstration project approach for his bill. It was not consistent with the president's rhetoric, the declaration of "total war" on poverty. The coordination or coalition approach was probably what most of the BOB representatives had in mind. The BOB is concerned with obtaining maximum effectiveness from federal dollars and viewed the coordination associated with community action agencies (CAAs) as a means for achieving this end. However, it is also likely that many of the drafters in the executive branch saw the CAAs as an instrument for increasing the political influence of the poor.

Moynihan has argued that the now famous "maximum feasible participation" provision was not intended to achieve this end. He has declared that

> Subsequently this phrase was taken to sanction a specific theory of social change, and there were those present in Washington at the time who would have drafted just such language with precisely that object. But the record, such as can be had, and recollection indicates that it was intended to do no more than ensure that persons excluded from the political process in the South and elsewhere would nonetheless participate in the benefits of the community action programs of the new legislation. It was taken as a matter beneath notice that such programs would be dominated by the local political structure.[22]

However, despite Moynihan's recollections and assertions, the record, such as it is, does provide evidence that the majority of the task force did have in mind the specific theory of social change we described as the political strategy. A study of the origin of the maximum feasible participation concept completed in 1966 and based largely on interviews with task force members found that the provision was argued for by Richard Boone, a veteran of the Ford Foundation and PCJD programs, and was accepted by the drafters with the full intention that the poor would begin to develop

37

organizations that could speak for them and effect change in community institutions.[23] John Donovan, a Johnson Administration official involved in preparing the bill, has also supported the interpretation that the PCJD staff presented this theory of social change and secured support for it from Shriver and his associates.[24] Finally, there is the testimony of Adam Yarmolinsky, who worked closely with Shriver and who was scheduled to become deputy director of OEO. Writing about "The Beginnings of OEO" he states that Boone continually argued for the necessity of involving the poor in order to achieve change and recalls,

> At one point during the February 4 brainstorming session, when Boone had used the phrase "maximum feasible participation" several times, this writer recalls saying to him, "You have used that phrase four or five times now." "Yes, I know," he replied. "How many more times do I have to use it before it becomes part of the program?" "Oh, a couple of times more," was the response. He did and it did.[25]

Thus it is clear that some of the drafters of the legislation had in mind a particular strategy when they prepared Title II of the EOA, and when several of the drafters (including Boone) were appointed to administrative positions in the newly created OEO they began to implement this theory. However, one must note that this approach was never clearly explained to or appreciated by congressmen when they initially endorsed the legislation.

It was mentioned earlier that Congress passed the bill within five months with only minor alterations and with virtually no change in Title II. The legislators lack of interest in this title is probably best explained by their failure to comprehend the nature of the program. During the hearings only one administration official sought to explain the meaning of the community action approach and none of the representatives pursued the explanation with follow-up questions. Robert Kennedy, then attorney general, told the Congress that community action "must be a total effort to bring about broad community change. And this cannot be done by the Federal Government. We can only help by stimulating local action. It must be done by local people and local agencies working closely together."[26]

Sar Levitan has noted with respect to Kennedy's testimony and Moynihan's later writings,

> In retrospect it is not surprising that Kennedy was the only federal official to attempt an explanation of the CAP concept. As chairman of the Cabinet Committee on Juvenile Delinquency, he was exposed to the nascent community action efforts funded by the federal government. Apparently, other Administrative spokesmen were quite innocent of CAP's meaning and had not been briefed by their departmental representatives on the task force that planned the legislation. Included among these latter were

some who later claimed to have predicted the future course of CAP.[27]

In sum it may be argued that some of the drafters of the EOA, who were drawn from the executive branch rather than Congress, were willing to accept the social theory underlying the political strategy and incorporated it in Title II of the Act. This portion of the bill was adopted by Congress with little debate. Members of the group that inititated the legislation later moved into administrative positions at OEO and began to implement this strategy. The initial implementation of the strategy led Congress, and perhaps the administrators themselves, to a fuller understanding of the meaning of community action. Undoubtedly, this understanding led many members of Congress to oppose the way in which OEO was executing its legislative mandate. Nonetheless, Title II of the EOA did represent, at least for a time, an opportunity to try the political strategy under a federal program. It is our purpose in a subsequent chapter to evalute the impact of Title II insofar as it followed the political stragegy.

NOTES

1. This section relies primarily upon Sar Levitan, *Federal Aid to Depressed Areas* (Baltimore: The Johns Hopkins Press, 1964); Garth Mangum, *The Emergence of Manpower Policy* (New York: Holt, Rinehart & Winston, 1969); James Sundquist, *Politics and Policy: The Eisenhower, Kennedy and Johnson Years* (Washington, D.C.: The Brookings Institution, 1968), Chapter III.

2. Sundquist surmises it was because of the speaker's longstanding objection to joint congressional-presidential committees on any subject. See Sundquist, *Politics and Policy*, p. 79.

3. U.S. Congress, Senate, Special Committee on Unemployment Problems, *Hearings, Studies in Unemployment, Readings in Unemployment,* and *Report No. 1206,* prepared pursuant to Senate Resolution 196, 86th Cong., 2d sess. 1960.

4. U.S. Congress, *Report No. 1206,* p. 124.

5. For a sensible discussion of this intradisciplinary dispute among economists, see Wilbur Thompson, *A Preface to Urban Economics* (Baltimore: The Johns Hopkins Press, 1968), pp. 204-13. The basic theory is explained in most introductory economics texts, the most famous of which is Paul Samuelson, *Economics: An Introductory Analysis* (New York: McGraw-Hill, 1971). For examples of congressional testimony reflecting the dispute see statements by Walter Heller and Charles Killingsworth in U.S. Congress, Senate, Hearings Before the Subcommittee on Employment, Manpower, and Poverty of the Committee on Labor and Public Welfare, *Nation's Manpower Revolution,* Part 5, 88th Cong., 1st sess. 1963, pp. 1461-511 and 1751-966.

6. Testimony of William B. Logan, President, American Vocational Association, in U.S. Congress, Senate, Subcommittee on Employment, Manpower, and Poverty of the Labor and Public Welfare Committee, 87th Cong., 1st Sess., 1961, *Training the Unemployed,* Hearings, p. 180.

7. *Ibid.*

8. Eli Ginzberg, *Manpower Advice for Government: National Manpower Advisory Committee Letters, 1962-1971* (Washington, D.C.: Government Printing Office, 1972), p. 12.

9. Testimony of Secretary of Labor W. Willard Wirtz in U.S. Congress, House, *Manpower Development and Training Act,* Hearings Before the Select Subcommittee on Labor of the House Education and Labor Committee, 88th Cong., 1st sess., p. 15.

10. *Manpower Report of the President,* U.S. Department of Labor, March 1966 (Washington, D.C., 1966), p. xv.

11. "Annual Message to the Congress on the State of the Union," January 17, 1968, *Public Papers of the Presidents of the United States, Lyndon B. Johnson, 1968-69* (Washington, D.C., 1970), Book One, p. 28.

12. "To Earn a Living: The Right of Every American," Special Message to Congress, January 23, 1968, *Public Papers of the Presidents of the United States, Lyndon B. Johnson, 1968-69,* p. 49.

13. This section relies primarily upon Sar Levitan, *The Design of Federal Anti-Poverty Strategy* (Ann Arbor, Mich.: Institute of Labor and Industrial Relations, 1967), which was reprinted as chapter 1 in Sar Levitan, *The Great Society's Poor Law: A New Approach to Poverty* (Baltimore: The Johns Hopkins Press, 1969), and Sundquist, *Politics and Policy,* chapter IV; also John Bibby and Roger Davidson, *On Capitol Hill: Studies in the Legislative Process* (New York: Holt, Rinehart and Winston, 1967), chapter 7; and Robert Levine, *The Poor Ye Need Not Have With You* (Cambridge: Massachusetts Institute of Technology Press, 1970), chapter 4.

14. Levitan, *Great Society's Poor Law,* p. 12.

15. Sundquist, *Politics and Policy,* pp. 111-14.

16. See Arthur Schlesinger, Jr., *A Thousand Days: John F. Kennedy in the White House* (Greenwich: Fawcett Crest, 1965), pp. 920-25; and Theodore Sorensen, *Kennedy* (New York: Bantam Books, 1965), p. 848.

17. As quoted in Levitan, *Great Society's Poor Law,* p. 17.

18. "The Annual State of the Union Message to Congress," January 8, 1964, reprinted in *A Time for Action: A Selection from the Speeches and Writings of Lyndon B. Johnson, 1953-1964* (New York: Atheneum, 1964), p. 168.

19. Edwin Witte, "Administrative Agencies and Statute Lawmaking," *Public Administration Review* 2, no. 2, reprinted in Claude Hawley and Ruth Weintraub, *Administrative Questions and Political Answers* (Princeton, N.J.: Van Nostrand, 1966), p. 150.

20. Bibby and Davidson, *On Capitol Hill,* p. 220.

21. Peter Marris and Martin Rein, *Dilemmas of Social Reform: Poverty and Community Action in the United States* (New York: Atherton Press, 1967).

22. Daniel P. Moynihan, *Maximum Feasible Misunderstanding: Community Action in the War on Poverty* (New York: The Free Press, 1969), p. 87.

23. Brian Smith, "The Role of the Poor in the Poverty Program: The Origin and Development of Maximum Feasible Participation" (unpublished M.A. thesis, Department of Public Law and Government, Columbia University, 1966), pp 11-12 and 20-22.

24. John Donovan, *The Politics of Poverty* (New York: Pegasus, 1967). esp. pp. 29-33.

25. Adam Yarmolinsky, "The Beginnings of OEO," in James Sundquist, ed., *On Fighting Poverty* (New York: Basic Books, 1969), p. 51.

26. U.S. Congress, House Committee on Education and Labor, *Hearings on Economic Opportunity Act,* 88th Cong., 2nd sess., Part 1, p. 304.

27. Levitan, *Great Society's Poor Law,* p. 110.

4

FRAMEWORK FOR ANALYSIS
OF ANTIPOVERTY POLICY IMPACTS

Study of the impact of government policies and of federal programs requires a framework within which to assemble and evaluate the available data. Each of the antipoverty strategies is predicated upon specified relationships between outputs of the political system in the form of some type of government intervention and selected environmental characteristics. The political strategy hypothesizes that intervention in the form of support for indigenous groups representing those at the lower end of the income distribution will alter local political decision-making patterns. The new political relationships will eventually result in an altered income distribution. The service strategy, as represented by the training programs, hypothesizes that government intervention in the form of vocational training for disadvantaged members of the labor force will enable them to increase their earnings from employment. Analysis of the impact of each of these strategies requires that we have a framework that specifies the evidence to be used to evaluate each strategy.

MANPOWER TRAINING AND THE SERVICE STRATEGY

Recent evaluations of manpower training efforts have generally followed a cost-benefit approach. These studies specify and quantify the costs incurred and benefits received from a specific program and then compute a cost-benefit ratio. Generally costs include the salaries of instructors, rent for classrooms, purchases of equipment, and similar items; benefits consist primarily of the added income graduates earn because of their new skills.

When the ratio is greater than 1 (benefits exceed costs) a program is said to be worthwhile. When a cost-benefit ratio is less than 1, it is assumed that simple transfer payments (cash allowance) would be more effective, and the program is considered a poor choice for government expenditures.[1]

By 1972 the cost-benefit literature relating to manpower training programs was extensive enough to have generated its own bibliographic material.[2] Among the most frequently cited cost-benefit studies are those drawing data from training activities in Massachusetts,[3] West Virginia,[4] Connecticut,[5] Michigan,[6] and North Carolina.[7] Follow-up data on trainee earnings, but no cost-benefit ratios, were provided in a comparative study of four cities[8] and in two national surveys.[9]

The several studies have produced cost-benefit ratios varying from 137:1 to 0.2:1. To a large degree these variations are explained by the differing definitions of costs and benefits and the differing assumptions under which the author computed his ratio. Examples of these differences include the presence or absence of control-group comparisons in computing benefits, allowance or nonallownace of earnings forgone by trainees during the training period in computing costs, and projection in calculating benefits of income gains over periods varying from 10 years to a lifetime. As the examples suggest, there are no generally agreed-upon rules for determining costs and benefits.

Efforts have been made by Einar Hardin and Thomas Ribich[10] to standardize the findings of the several cost-benefit studies by applying uniform computational rules to the raw data. These procedures significantly reduce the variation in cost-benefit ratios but still leave a range of 0.2:1 to 17.3:1.[11] However, the smallest figure is based upon long and costly courses in one program in Michigan, and there is general agreement that the over-all cost-benefit ratio for most types of training is greater than 1.

But the computation of a cost-benefit ratio is not suitable as an evaluation of training as an antipoverty strategy. Cost-benefit calculations include all benefits, regardless of who receives them. Benefits are typically defined as increases in gross national product resulting from the increased productivity of trainees (and reflected in their earnings) and the reduction in transfer payments made possible by this increased productivity. The basis of cost-benefit calculations is total gains to the economy from investment in training, not necessarily the distribution of these gains among the various segments of the population.

The inappropriateness of cost-benefit ratios is best illustrated by the fact that they count income gains from training for the nonpoor as well as for the poor. If the objective of a program is to alleviate poverty, it is inconsistent to count as a benefit of this program all the income gains achieved by those individuals with family incomes above predetermined poverty levels. Ribich has suggested that a range be established between a minimum poverty line and a maximum poverty line. Income gains that bring a person to the minimum poverty line would be given full weight in benefit computations; income gains bringing a family's income to levels between the minimum and maximum poverty lines would be given decreasing weight; and gains above the maximum level would be counted as zero.[12] However, calculations of this type require far more detailed data than is presently available, and Ribich did not try to apply the above schema when evaluating training programs.

Because of its inappropriateness as a tool in antipoverty policy evaluation, a gross cost-benefit approach will not be followed in this study. Rather we shall seek to trace the impact of the programs upon their clients. The analysis shall depend primarily upon data gathered by program administrators. In our analysis of the data, answers to three key questions will be sought:

(1) To what extent are the services being utilized by the target population? The concern is with what Burton Weisbrod has called a program's "vertical target efficiency," that is, the "degree to which a program intended to benefit a low-income Group A also benefits a higher income Group B."[13] If a program designed to benefit the poor is also used by many who are "nonpoor," the program's vertical efficiency may be quite low. If training services intended for the most disadvantaged members of the labor force are being utilized by those who are already in a relatively good position to compete for desirable jobs (for example, high school graduates), then the training programs have a low vertical efficiency. We shall consciously ignore what Weisbrod terms the "horizontal target efficiency," which "is the degree to which a program intended to benefit Group A reaches all members of this group."[14] The horizontal efficiency of anti-poverty programs gauges the extent to which all individuals who are "poor" (however defined) are served by the program. If half the poor heads of households enroll in training, then the training programs have a horizontal efficiency of 50 percent. Horizontal efficiency will not be considered in this study because it is recognized that antipoverty policy is still in an experimental stage and no single program pretends to deal with the total problem. In fact, the purpose and spirit of this inquiry is to view the efforts of the 1960s as social experiments and to determine which type or types of program appear to be most effective. It was not intended, and it is not expected, that any single antipoverty program would have complete horizontal efficiency.

(2) To what extent is the target population able to complete training successfully? This question is considered for two reasons: First, it is possible that many enrollees are drawn from the target population, but only a few complete the program. The program must be judged, in part, by its suitability to the target population. Second, income gains associated with training can be attributed to training only if an enrollee has completed the program. Training programs are generally of short duration aimed at the acquisition of specific skills. Unlike general education there is not a

continuous range within which to judge an individual's level of preparation. Generally one is either trained or not for a particular job. Income gains achieved by enrollees who do not satisfactorily complete training should not be attributed to the training program, and it is important to take cognizance of this in assessing the program's impact.

(3) To what extent does training result in added income for members of the target population who enroll in and complete a program? This is the most important aspect of the evaluation, for it deals with the crucial variable of income. It should be determined if successful training of the poor enables them to achieve higher incomes than would otherwise be the case. It should be kept in mind that if a program has limited vertical efficiency, only a small percentage of the enrollee population will be from the target population. Only the income changes of this segment of the enrollee population should be considered. It is theoretically possible that a program with a high cost-benefit ratio but a low vertical efficiency will be an ineffective antipoverty program.

COMMUNITY ACTION AND THE POLITICAL STRATEGY

The impact of community action programs is not as easily assessed as that of manpower training programs. Analysis must rely upon examination of what former OEO Research Director Robert Levine called "proximate" effects. Levine has defined proximate effects, using as an example health programs:

> Each program evaluated has both proximate and ultimate effects. The proximate effects are those which a program has upon its immediate objective—an antipoverty health program upon the objective of improving the health of the poor, for example. The evaluation of the ultimate effects is that which measures the program's effects against the overall program objectives— effectiveness of the health programs as a means of decreasing poverty through improvements of the productive capacity of the poor.[15]

Levine goes on to point out that for manpower training programs proximate and ultimate benefits are similar—increased earnings from training have a direct effect upon income levels. Evaluation in such cases is more direct than in a case where proximate and ultimate objectives are not identical. The Community Action Program, to the extent that it represents the political strategy, has as its proximate goal the improvement of the position of low-income groups in the decision-making structure of their local community. In examining the program we shall concentrate upon this proximate effect.

The analysis of community decision-making comprises a substantial body of literature in the fields of sociology and political science. The common threads in many of these studies have been a series of controversies over the proper methodology for analyzing community power structures, the extent to which community decision-making is dominated by a single elite, and the degree to which political resources are dispersed among participants. Each of these questions should be discussed as a background for formulating a framework in which to assess the impact of community action programs on local decision-making.

It should be noted at the outset of this discussion that the terms "decision-making structures" and "power structures" will be used interchangeably. This is so because our working definition of power is that specified by Lasswell and Kaplan:

> Power is participation in the making of decisions: G has power over H with respect to the values K if G participates in the making of decisions affecting the K-policies of H.[16]

This definition of power does not conform completely with the definition of some of the students of community power. Often the concept of power resembles that specified by Dahl. He defines power as "coercive influence," exemplified as follows: "A influences B to the extent that he gets B to do something that B would not otherwise do."[17] As James March has noted in an analytic essay, "The Power of Power,"[18] this latter conception of power represents formidable obstacles to research, including the distinction between actual or exercised power and potential power as well as determining the hypothetical condition of "what B would otherwise have done." Power defined in Dahl's terms embraces much more than the participation in decision-making, but because of the formidable conceptual problems related to adopting his definition we shall limit ourselves to an interpretation of power as participation in decision-making.

Arnold Rose has divided the methods for studying community power into three categories: the positional approach, the reputational approach, and the decision-making approach.[19] The positional approach identifies the power structure with formal roles in established institutions. It rests on the assumption that formal position is correlated with power. However, since the development of this approach, it has become generally recognized that informal structures are at least as significant as formal ones. Consequently, the positional approach, by itself, is generally regarded as inadequate and is now rarely employed in community-power studies.

Those using the reputational approach construct a model of the power structure based upon the judgments of community members who are considered well-informed about the community's political life. The best-known reputational study, one that has been the basis for much later work, is Floyd Hunter's *Community Power Structure*.[20] Hunter described the power structure in Atlanta, Georgia, by asking a carefully selected panel of 14 "judges" from within the community to name the "top leaders" in the city. This effort resulted in a list of 40 "top influentials," and interviews with these 40 produced a list of 12 "upper limits personnel." This latter group was seen as the elite group that made decisions for the community and delegated decision-making authority to those under them.

The proponents of the decision-making approach believe power structures can best be identified by studying participation in decisions rather than reputations for influence or lists of incumbents in top positions in formal organizations. They study the characteristics of those who participate in key decisions and from this evidence extract a picture of the community's power structure. Nelson Polsby has described the mechanics of the process as follows: "First, the researcher should pick issue-areas as the focus of his study of community power. Secondly, he should be able to defend these issue-areas as very important in the life of the community. Thirdly, he should study actual behavior, either at first hand or by reconstructing behavior from documents, informants, newspapers and other appropriate sources."[21] Among the better-known studies using the approach are those by Dahl, Banfield, and Martin and associates.[22]

The decision-making approach has been criticized on methodological ground by Peter Bachrach and Morton Baratz.[23] They specify two major defects of the decision-making approach: "One is that the model takes no account of the fact that power may be, and often is, exercised by confining the scope of decision-making to relatively 'safe' issues. The other is that the model provides no objective criteria for distinguishing between 'important' and 'unimportant' issues arising in the political arena."[24] To overcome these defects Bachrach and Baratz urged that researchers pay attention to non-decision, defined as "a decision that results in suppression or thwarting of a latent or manifest challenge to the values or interests of the decision makers. To be more nearly explicit, non-decision-making is a means by which demands for change in the existing allocation of benefits and privileges in the community can be suffocated before they are even voiced."[25]

Richard Merelman has criticized the nondecision-making framework on the grounds that "nondecisions" are "nonevents" that are not subject to empirical verification and, therefore, to objective study.[26] Bachrach and Baratz reply that "although absence of conflict may be a nonevent, a decision which results in prevention of conflict is very much an event—and an observable one to boot."[27] Nondecisions can be studied by first asking, "What persons or groups in the community are especially disfavored under the existing distribution of benefits and privileges?"[28] Then the investigator must determine what the grievances of the disfavored groups are and "why and by what means some or all of the potential demands for change have been denied airing."[29]

The problem of the "researchability" of nondecisions has been given further consideration in articles by Raymond Wolfinger and Frederick

Frey.[30] Both agree that "analysts of policy formation who limit their attention to overt conflict miss many exercises of power."[31] However, Wolfinger is less optimistic than Frey about the possibilities of empirically determining the incidence and nature of nondecisions. Wolfinger presents the problem as follows:

> The core of the problem is the difficulty of identifying non-decisions, which seems generally to come back to determining peoples' "real interest" as opposed to what they say they want or what they are trying to get through political action. . . . What criteria can be developed to guide the researcher to nondecisions *before* they become part of the political agenda? Specifically, how can bona fide examples of nonparticipation and absention be distinguished from the common apathy and lack of public spirit that characterize political life. The student of political power cannot be expected to concern himself with every event that might happen but has not yet come to pass; he needs guidelines to know *which* nonevents to study.[32]

Frey has suggested three types of guidelines that might help resolve the problem of the researchability of nondecisions. The three tools for developing expectations about influence relationships are theory, comparison, and analysis of "who benefits" from policy outputs. Although Frey finds existing theories of political participation "rudimentary" he feels the theory of interest-group participation is slightly more advanced and that "these scattered nuggets need to be integrated under a more comprehensive theoretical perspective, but even now it is possible in limited areas for us to present many rough but useful hypotheses about how the various actors in a community will try to exert influence."[33] With respect to the usefulness of comparison, Frey cites Mathew Cranson's study of air pollution and points out that if six of seven cities with similar air pollution levels display protest movements, then one should examine the nonissue in the seventh. Finally, Frey is cautious about using "who benefits" type of analysis for identifying nonissues but still maintains it can be a "useful clue." Thus through a judicious mixture of these three tools political scientists can explore non-decisions in local communities.

Along with the methodological controversy there has been a dispute over substantive findings. Several studies have found that communities are dominated by a single cohesive group, usually comprised of business leaders. Hunter's study exemplifies such findings. As noted earlier, he found there was a group of men who interacted socially and made decisions for the community and that "the test for admission to this circle of decision-makers is almost wholly a man's position in the business community."[34] In contrast, other studies have found different patterns of participation in decision-making. Dahl's study of New Haven found several important types of participants, each active in different areas of decision-making. There was no single group (or elite) that exercised universal control.[35] A similar pattern was found in Syracuse.[36]

Sayre and Kaufman's study of New York found that there were not only several different groups active in different areas but that even within specific issue areas no single set of participants was continuously dominant. This summary of the situation in New York is typical of "pluralist" findings:

> So in our judgment, it remains true that no single ruling elite controls the political and governmental system of New York City. The system is still characterized by numerous decision centers, each populated by a constellation of core groups and their satellites, each active with respect to a limited set of political and governmental decisions, each comparatively indifferent to the decisions that emanate from other centers except when these impinge forcefully on their own interests, and each arriving at decisions in its sphere of interest through bargaining among its constituent elements .... In a broad sense, then, it may be said that nobody "runs" New York; it runs by a process of negotiation and mutual accommodation, with all the virtues and weaknesses such a process entails.[37]

Other studies of New York City have confirmed the finding of numerous decision (or issue) areas but indicate that each is dominated by a single cohesive group rather than characterized by bargaining among rival participants. Theodore Lowi's study of the appointment process found that political parties no longer held a monopoly over all such decisions but that within four broad policy areas appointments were dominated by individuals drawn from uniform and identifiable recruitment channels.[38] Robb Burlage's study of health and hospital policy in New York City found this issue area was dominated by a select group of medical school leaders with common interests,[39] but a later study by Ginzberg and associates found greater pluralism.[40] Marilyn Gittell's study of educational decision-making in New York City found that the process was dominated by professional educators performing administrative functions at the Board of Education's headquarters.[41]

Related to the controversy over the diversity of participation in any issue area is the question of distribution of political resources among potentially competing participants. The list of political resources is extensive. Polsby has compiled a suggestive list that includes money and credit, patronage, information, social status, popularity, legitimacy, solidarity or orgaization, and energetic leadership.[42]

The dominant position of a group within an issue area may result from its ability to win out consistently over others in the decision process because the group has superior political resources. If there are several participants active in a policy area but resources are not evenly distributed among them, then it is possible for one group to assume a dominant position. Evidence indicates this is the case in urban renewal decisions in many cities. Summing up a variety of case studies [43] of such decisions, Scott Greer has concluded, "The residents of declining neighborhoods have very little might in the decisions. . . . They are usually neighborhoods of the bottom dogs; they lack expertise, organizational skills, and association with the powerful."[44] In contrast, those who achieve their objectives in urban renewal decisions possess substantial political resources. They are "mayors concerned with increasing central city tax base, civic leaders with a patriotic desire 'to make our city center beautiful,' businessmen with deep commitments to downtown real estate, and those who believe government would innovate in the public interest."[45]

However, it is also possible that the domination of a group in any particular issue area results from the fact that it is the only class of participant active in that area. The ability of a small group of party leaders to control political nominations in New Haven appears to fall into this category. Dahl's description of the process is as follows:

> But even the enrolled party members rarely use their legal right to participate in nominations. The turnout for the caucuses and ward primaries in which ward leaders are elected is usually negligible; often only the ward leaders show up, accompanied perhaps by a few members of the nominating committee. Rank and file opposition to the nominations made by the leaders is virtually unknown; in the absence of a faction of dissident subleaders in the party, the rank and file are unlikely to participate at all in the nominating process.[46]

As a third alternative, political resources may be relatively evenly divided among participants in a policy area with the result that no single group consistently dominates the decision-making process. Sayre and Kaufman believe that this arrangement characterizes most issue areas in New York City. They conclude their discussion of nongovernmental groups by stating:

> The system functions in such a way that anyone who feels strongly enough about any govermental decision need not feel, or be, extremely alienated; the statement, "You can't fight City Hall!" does not describe the governmental process that now obtains in New York. For any group can fight City Hall, almost every group does, and many are remarkably effective.[47]

The controversies over the nature of community power structures provide a basis for constructing a framework within which to evaluate the

Community Action Program. To the extent that the program embraces the political strategy described in Chapter 1, it seeks to alter community decision-making patterns so that the poor enjoy a more favorable position. This improved position may be achieved in one or more of three ways.

First, grievances or proposals formerly subject to non-decision-making may become subject to open discussion and settlement or negotiation within the decision-making structures. For example, policies affecting the treatment of minority groups or the incidence of poverty may move from the realm of private concerns and individual action to fall within the scope of formal decision-making processes.

Second, the diversity of participation within one or more policy arenas in which representation of the poor had formerly been absent might be broadened to include such groups. An example would be the formation of a caucus to nominate independent (nonorganization) candidates for office in the political parties in New Haven described by Dahl.

Finally, participants representing poor constituents might acquire added resources so that in cases where they formerly participated but did not prevail or achieve satisfactory bargaining outcomes, they are now able to achieve more favorable treatment. To again refer to our original examples, such a transformation might be a successful fight by slum residents to block an urban renewal project, when they had formerly been unable to do so.

In sum, the study of community decision-making points to three critical dimensions along which we can assess the impact of community action intervention—the transformation of grievances from non-decision-making to active consideration, the participation of the poor in issue areas where they formerly did not play a role, and the provision of additional resources to poverty groups, so they might participate more effectively in areas previously concerning them.

DATA AND METHODS

The preceding sections have set forth an analytic framework within which to assess the impact of strategies and programs. The next step is to specify the nature of the data to be used and the methods whereby they were gathered. Data to assess the impact of manpower training programs were obtained from the following sources: (1) the *Manpower Report of the President*—a document issued annually, which contains a statistical appendix providing selected information on federal manpower programs; (2) the annual reports prepared by the Secretary of Health, Education, and Welfare on the training programs authorized by Title II of the MDTA (institutional training). These reports to Congress are required by Section 233 of the act and contain figures on institutional training programs; (3) congressional hearings on the passage of MDTA in 1962 and amendments to the act in 1963 and 1966; (4)

congressional hearings on the annual appropriations for manpower programs, which are part of the Department of Labor's annual appropriation; (5) research studies prepared under grants or contracts from the Department of Labor and dealing with the effectiveness of manpower programs; all such studies completed or under progress are listed each year by the Department of Labor in its annual publication *Manpower Research and Development Projects;* and (6) administrative data obtained from the Office of Manpower, Management Data Systems, Manpower Administration, U.S. Department of Labor.

Data to assess the CAP were drawn from both primary and secondary sources. The secondary sources consist of the published studies dealing with one or more community action programs. The studies have been analyzed and interpreted in accord with the framework detailed in an earlier section of this chapter. Other sources include (1) congressional hearings entitled *Examination of the War on Poverty,* which review the experience of several community action programs; (2) annual reports issued by the Community Action Program, Office of Economic Opportunity; (3) research studies dealing with the Community Action Program conducted under contract with the Office of Economic Opportunity. The OEO contract studies, unlike similar DOL studies, are not listed in any publication and are not available for even limited distribution. Access to the unpublished studies was obtained through visits to the national office of OEO in Washington and to the New York office of Daniel Yankelovich, Inc., a private research firm.

QUASI-EXPERIMENTAL RESEARCH DESIGN
AND PROBLEMS OF EVALUATION

Both the political strategy and the service strategy are based upon the assumption that governmental intervention, in one form or another, will have an impact on selected societal problems. But societies are dynamic and constantly undergoing changes.[48] The difficulty in assessing the impact of any single program is in determining whether an observed change results from a particular intervention or not.

Donald Campbell and Julian Stanley have identified 12 potential sources of invalidity that arise in making cause and effect judgments about the effects of a particular independent variable.[49] The 12 are intended to assist designers of research experiments in the education field, but 4 are especially relevant to the analysis of antipoverty programs. In drawing conclusions about antipoverty policy, one must be aware of these sources of invalidity.

First, *history* or the specific events occurring at the time of the introduction or implementation of some specific form of government intervention may be the source of change. For example, Harold Sheppard in an article on "Some Broader Reality Frameworks for Antipoverty Intervention" points out that the War on Poverty was waged during a period of deficit spending, tax reductions, and capital investment credits and that these and other broad trends must be considered in evaluating the impact of particular programs.[50] In experimental designs the best way to allow for the effects of history is to use a control group, but *post hoc* research on poverty programs does not always permit this. Consequently, in making judgments about the impact of programs we must take into consideration the effects of other concurrent events.

A second potential source of invalidity is what Campbell and Stanley call *maturation.* This refers to "processes within the respondents operating as a function of the passage of time per se (not specific to the particular events)."[51] An example of the importance of this factor can be seen in evaluations of the Neighborhood Youth Corps, a federal program with the proclaimed goals of enhancing the employability of youths. When consideration is given to the fact that teenagers' unemployment rates normally decline as teenagers mature, the impact of the government intervention in the form of counseling, supplemental education, and work experience may be negligible. This has led most evaluators to conclude that the program's major function, aside from income transfers to poor youths, is the provision of an "aging vat" in which youths can mature.[52]

The problem of *differential selection* arises when control groups are used to eliminate the difficulties arising from the factors of history and maturation. In many experimental situations careful selection of control groups can reduce or eliminate the effects of differential selection. But the operations of most government programs do not allow random assignments to control groups. Thus, even when control groups are incorporated into program evaluation designs, it is possible that some important noncontrolled factor may distinguish the experimental group. This difficulty is prominent in the evaluation of training programs where it is likely that graduates and those frequently used as control groups (usually either dropouts or others with socioeconomic characteristics similar to those of enrollees) differ in key psychological characteristics such as motivation and career orientation that are likely to affect their labor market experiences.

The fourth source of invalidity that may distort policy analyses is the of *experimental mortality,* defined as a differential loss of respondents between control and experimental groups. Examples of instances in which this factor may be operative are found in the evaluation of training programs where enrollees and controls are compared. These enrollees who drop out or experience difficulty securing employment after training are likely to be less responsive to follow-up questionnaires or interviews. This may affect the evaluation by biasing the data in favor of more successful trainees.

Many efforts aimed at evaluating social-action programs have not been able to deal successfully with the potential sources of invalidity inherent in quasi-experimental research. Peter Rossi's review of a sample of 200 evaluation studies funded by the OEO found that "not a single report contained by the most charitable definition the results of a controlled experiment."[53]   Rossi also observed,

> Nor is this a peculiarity of Poverty Program researches. Research on the effects of educational programs, on the effectiveness of police methods, even on the effectiveness of publicity campaigns all have the same characteristic of falling short of the potentialities of currently acceptable research methodology. Evaluating the effectiveness of social-action programs is a depressed area within the realm of behavioral science.[54]

Robert Weiss and Martin Rein have argued that valid quasi-experimental designs are virtually impossible to implement in the evaluation of social programs because of both technical and administrative problems.[55]   In addition to the technical problems described by Stanley and Campbell, they also identify administrative problems including the tendency of operationalized criteria to become goals in themselves and changes in personnel and program content over time. Weiss and Rein admit that their article "is for the most part an essay in destructive criticism. The more constructive parallel essay on the methods of research which could be appropriate for the study of the effects of broad-aim programs would be more difficult to write, because there are fewer models to use."[56]   However, the authors do provide two general guidelines for improved research technique: first, the use of more descriptive data and inductive techniques, and, second, the adoption of a systems perspective that would focus on relationships between the program and the existing system. Little elaboration is provided on the proposed guidelines, and they note that "there are, indeed, problems of many sorts associated with nonexperimental approaches, including the mechanics of data production, the methods of organizing and analyzing data, and the logic of generalization." But Weiss and Rein conclude that "the way to develop the methodology, we believe, is to begin working at it."[57]

Pending the development of a new and more appropriate methodology, the best way to assess the impact of antipoverty programs continues to be the gathering of data in a systematic fashion that seeks to avoid the sources of invalidity described by Stanley and Campbell. At the same time we may keep in mind the difficulties and guidelines suggested by Weiss and Rein and seek descriptive data of the type they suggest where quasi-experimental designs seem impractical or impossible.

NOTES

1. See Garth Mangum, "Determining the Results of Manpower and Anti-Poverty Programs," in U.S. Congress, Joint Economic Committee, *The Analysis and Evaluation of Public Expenditures: The PPB System*, vol. 3 (Washington, D.C., 1969), pp. 1171-80.

2. W. D. Wood and H. F. Wood, *Cost Benefit Analysis and the Economics of Investment in Human Resources: An Annotated Bibliography* (Kingston, Ont.: Industrial Relations Centre, Queens University, 1970); and U.S. Congress, Joint Economic Committee, Subcommittee on Fiscal Policy, *The Effectiveness of Manpower Training Programs: A Review of Research on the Impact on the Poor* (Washington, D.C. 1972).

3. David A. Page, "Retraining Under the Manpower Development Act: A Cost-Benefit Analysis," *Public Policy* 13, pp. 257-67.

4. Gerald Somers and Ernst Stromsdorfer, "A Benefit-Cost Analysis of Manpower Retraining," in Gerald Somers, ed., *Proceedings of the 17th Annual Meeting,* Industrial Relations Research Association (Madison, Wis., 1965), pp. 172-85; Harold Gibbard and G. Somers, "Government Retraining of the Unemployed in West Virginia," in G. Somers, ed., *Retraining the Unemployed* (Madison: University of Wisconsin Press, 1968), pp. 17-124; Glen Cain and Ernst Stromsdorfer, "An Economic Evaluation of Government Retraining Programs in West Virginia," in Somers, ed., *Retraining the Unemployed,* pp. 290-335; and E. Stromsdorfer, "Determinants of Economic Success in Retraining the Unemployed," *Journal of Human Resources,* Spring 1968, pp. 139-58.

5. Michael E. Borus, "A Benefit-Cost Analysis of the Economic Effectiveness of Retraining the Unemployed," *Yale Economic Essays* (Fall 1964), 371-430; and Borus, "The Effects of Retraining the Unemployed in Connecticut," in Somers, ed., *Retraining the Unemployed* pp. 125-48.

6. Einar Hardin and M. Borus, *Economic Benefits and Costs of Retraining Courses in Michigan* (Washington, D.C.: U.S. Department of Labor, 1970).

7. D. O. Sewell, *Training the Poor* (Kingston, Ont.: Industrial Relations Centre, Queens University, 1971).

8. Olympus Research Corporation, "Total Impact Evaluation of Manpower Programs in Four Cities" (Washington, D.C., August 1971).

9. Decision Making Information, "MDTA Outcomes Study: Final Report" (Santa Ana, Cal., November 1971); and Earl Main, "A Nationwide Evaluation of MDTA Institutional Job Training," *Journal of Human Resources* (Spring 1968), pp. 97-118.

10. Einar Hardin, "Benefit-Cost Analysis of Occupational Training Programs: A Comparison of Recent Studies," in G. Somers and W. D. Woods, eds., *Cost Benefit Analysis of Manpower Policies,* Proceedings of a North American Conference, May 14-15, 1969 (Kingston, Ont.: Industrial Relations Centre, Queens University, 1969), pp. 97-118; and Thomas Ribich, *Education and Poverty* (Washington, D.C.: The Brookings Institution, 1968), pp. 38-50.

11. The figures are from Hardin, "Benefit-Cost Analysis of Occupational Training Programs," p. 113.

12. Ribich, *Education and Poverty,* pp. 29-33.

13. Burton Weisbrod, "Collective Action and the Distribution of Income: A Conceptual Approach," in U.S. Congress, Joint Economic Committee, *Analysis and Evaluation,* Vol. 1, p. 185.

14. *Ibid.*, p. 185.

15. Robert Levine, "Policy Analysis and Economic Opportunity Programs," U.S. Congress, Joint Economic Committee, *Analysis and Evaluation,* Vol. 3, p. 1190.

16. Harold Lasswell and Abraham Kaplan, *Power and Society: A Framework for Political Inquiry* (New Haven, Conn.: Yale University Press, 1950), p. 75.

17. Robert Dahl, *Modern Political Analysis* (Englewood Cliffs, N.J.: Prentice-Hall, 1963), p. 40.

18. James March, "The Power of Power," in David Easton, ed., *Varieties of Political Theory* (Englewood Cliffs, N.J.: Prentice-Hall, 1966), pp. 39-70.

19. Arnold Rose, *The Power Structure* (New York: Oxford University Press, 1967), pp. 255-280.

20. Floyd Hunter, *Community Power Structure* (New York: Doubleday, 1963).

21. Nelson Polsby, *Community Power and Political Theory* (New Haven, Conn.: Yale University Press, 1963), pp. 120-21.

22. Robert Dahl, *Who Governs?* (New Haven, Conn.: Yale University Press, 1961); Edward Banfield, *Political Influence* (Glencoe, Ill.: The Free Press, 1961); and Roscoe Martin *et al., Decisions in Syracuse* (Bloomington: Indiana University Press, 1961).

23. See P. Bachrach and M. Baratz, "Two Faces of Power," *American Political Science Review (APSR),* 56 (1962), pp. 947-52; "Decisions and Nondecisions: An Analytic Framework," *APSR* 57 (1963), pp. 641-51; "A Power Analysis: The Shaping of Anti-Poverty Policy in Baltimore," *Public Policy* (Winter 1970); *Power and Poverty: Theory and Practice* (New York: Oxford University Press, 1970).

24. Bachrach and Baratz, *Power and Poverty,* p. 6.

25. *Ibid.*, p. 44.

26. Richard Merelman,, "On the Neoelitist Critique of Community Power," *APSR* 62 (June 1968), 451-61.

27. Bachrach and Baratz, *Power and Poverty,* p. 46.

28. *Ibid.*, p. 50.

29. *Ibid.*, p. 49.

30. Raymond Wolfinger, "Nondecisions and the Study of Local Politics," and Frederick Frey, "Comment: On Issues and Nonissues in the Study of Power," and Raymond Wolfinger, "Rejoinder to Frey's 'Comment'," all in *APSR* 65, 4 (December 1971), 1063-1104.

31. Wolfinger, "Rejoinder to Frey's 'Comment'," p. 1102.

32. Wolfinger, "Nondecisions and the Study of Local Politics," pp. 1077-78.

33. Frey, "Comment: On Issues and Nonissues in the Study of Power," p. 1095.

34. Hunter, *Community Power Structure*, p. 78.

35. Dahl, *Who Governs?*

36. Martin *et al.*, *Decisions in Syracuse.*

37. Wallace Sayre and Herbert Kaufman, *Governing New York City: Politics in the Metropolis* (New York: W. W. Norton, 1965), pp. xl-xli.

38. Theordore Lowi, *At the Pleasure of the Mayor* (New York: The Free Press, 1964).

39. Robb Burlage, *New York City's Municipal Hospitals* (Washington, D.C.: Institute for Policy Studies, 1967); see also Health Policy Advisory Center, *The American Health Empire: Power, Politics and Profits* (New York: Random House, 1971).

40. Eli Ginzberg and the Conservation of Human Resources Staff, *Urban Health Services: The Case of New York* (New York: Columbia University Press, 1971).

41. Marilyn Gittell, *Participants and Participation* (New York: Center for Urban Education, 1966). See also David Rogers, *110 Livingston Street* (New York: Random House, 1968).

42. Polsby, *Community Power and Political Theory*, pp. 119-20. See also Dahl, *Who Governs?*, Book IV.

43. Book-length studies are Peter Rossi and Robert Dentler, *The Politics of Urban Renewal* (New York: The Free Press, 1961); Harold Kaplan, *Urban Renewal Politics: Slum Clearance in Newark* (New York: Columbia University Press, 1963); and Herbert Gans, *The Urban Villagers* (New York: The Free Press, 1962).

44. Scott Greer, *Urban Renewal and American Cities* (New York: Bobbs-Merrill, 1965), p. 120.

45. *Ibid.*, p. 122.

46. Dahl, *Who Governs?*, p. 109.

47. Sayre and Kaufman, *Governing New York City*, pp. 514-15.

48. See David Easton, *A Framework for Political Analysis* (Englewood Cliffs, N.J.: Prentice-Hall, 1965); or Talcott Parsons, *The Social System* (New York: The Free Press, 1964).

49. Donald Campbell and Julian Stanley, *Experimental and Quasi-Experimental Designs for Research* (Chicago: Rand McNally, 1963).

50. Harold Sheppard, "Some Broader Reality Frameworks for Anti-Poverty Intervention," *Social Science Quarterly*, December 1969, pp. 487-93.

51. Campbell and Stanley, *Experimental and Quasi-Experimental Designs for Research*, p. 5.

52. See *Neighborhood Youth Corps: A Review of Research*, U.S. Department of Labor, Manpower Administration, Research Monograph No. 13 (Washington, D.C., 1970); Sar Levitan and Garth Mangum, *Federal Training and Work Programs in the Sixties* (Ann Arbor, Mich.: Institute of Labor and Industrial Relations, 1966), chapter 5, pp. 211-34.

53. Peter Rossi, "Practice, Method and Theory in Evaluating Social Action Programs," in James Sundquist, ed., *On Fighting Poverty: Perspectives from Experience* (New York: Basic Books, 1969), p. 223.

54. *Ibid.*, p. 218.

55. Martin Rein and Robert Weiss, "The Evaluation of Broad-Aim Programs: A Cautionary Case and a Moral," *Annals*, September 1969, pp. 133-42.

56. *Ibid.*, pp. 141-42.

57. *Ibid.*, p. 142.

5

THE IMPACT
OF TRAINING
PROGRAMS

This chapter evaluates the impact of federal training programs as an antipoverty effort. The federal training programs to be considered are the MDTA institutional, MDTA on-the-job (OJT), and the Job Opportunities in the Business Sector (JOBS) programs. For each program the available evidence will be examined to determine if individuals below the officially defined poverty line have access to the available training and if they benefit from participating through greater earned income.

ENROLLMENT IN TRAINING

The first step in assessing the impact of federally funded training services is to determine to what extent the services reach the poor. As explained in Chapter 4, we shall use criteria of "vertical efficiency" rather than "horizontal efficiency." Tables 5.1 and 5.2 present the available national data on the characteristics of MDTA institutional and MDTA on-the-job trainees for fiscal years 1963 to 1971. It is interesting to note that among the data gathered by the Department of Labor (DOL) there is no indication of the poverty status of the enrollees. As explained in Chapter 2, definitions of poverty relate to family size and family income. Whether or not individuals with similar incomes fall below a specific poverty line depends on the size of their family and the additional income earned by their spouse or offspring. Data on individual earnings are not sufficient to

TABLE 5.1

**Characteristics of Trainees Enrolled in
MDTA Institutional Training Programs
(percent distribution)**

Characteristic	Total	1971	1970	1969	1968	1967	1966	1965	1964	1963
Total										
Number (thousands)	1,134.0	155.6	130.0	135.0	140.0	150.0	177.5	145.3	68.6	32.0
Percent	100.0	100.0	100.0	100.0	100.0	100.0	100.0	100.0	100.0	100.0
Sex										
Male	58.2	58.5	59.4	55.6	55.4	56.8	58.3	60.9	59.7	63.8
Female	41.8	41.5	40.6	44.4	44.6	43.2	41.7	39.1	40.3	36.2
Age										
Under 19 years	14.4	13.8	9.1	12.5	14.9	16.4	15.9	18.3	10.6	6.3
19 to 21 years	24.1	26.1	28.0	25.0	23.6	23.6	22.2	24.3	24.7	19.1
22 to 34 years	36.5	40.2	42.3	38.2	35.5	34.3	35.3	32.4	36.4	43.9
35 to 44 years	14.6	11.4	11.9	14.0	15.2	14.7	15.6	14.9	17.5	20.3
45 years and over	10.3	8.5	8.8	10.3	10.8	11.0	11.0	10.1	10.8	10.4
Race										
White	60.4	55.6	59.2	55.9	50.8	59.1	62.5	67.7	69.9	76.5
Black	36.3	39.3	36.0	39.7	45.4	38.0	35.2	30.1	28.3	21.4
Other	3.3	5.1	4.8	4.4	3.8	2.9	2.3	2.2	1.8	2.1

60

Education										
Under 8 years	7.2	5.4	6.4	9.0	9.2	7.5	6.7	8.1	5.7	3.1
8 years	9.3	7.0	8.2	9.8	10.0	10.7	9.6	10.2	8.4	7.6
9 to 11 years	36.8	36.2	38.1	38.8	40.6	38.9	35.7	34.1	33.3	30.0
12 years	41.0	45.4	42.7	37.9	34.7	38.0	42.0	41.8	45.2	50.4
Over 12 years	5.7	6.0	4.5	4.5	5.5	4.9	6.0	5.8	7.4	8.9
Public assistance recipient										
Yes	12.2	15.8	12.9	13.4	12.6	12.1	11.2	10.5	9.7	8.1
No	87.8	84.2	87.1	86.6	87.4	87.9	88.8	89.5	90.3	91.9
Prior employment status										
Unemployed	81.4	72.7	73.8	79.6	79.7	80.3	82.8	87.8	90.5	92.1
Other	18.6	27.3	26.2	20.4	20.3	19.7	17.2	12.2	9.5	7.9

Source: Manpower Report of the President 1972, Table F-5, p. 265.

TABLE 5.2

Characteristics of Trainees Enrolled in MDTA-OJT Programs
(percent distribution)

Characteristic	Total	1970	1969	1968	1967	1966	1965	1964	1963
Total									
Number (thousands)	473.0	91.0	85.0	101.0	115.0	58.3	11.6	9.0	2.1
Percent	100.0	100.0	100.0	100.0	100.0	100.0	100.0	100.0	100.0
Sex									
Male	67.9	65.9	65.1	68.4	67.0	72.0	71.9	70.9	80.8
Female	32.1	34.1	34.9	31.6	33.0	28.0	28.1	29.1	19.2
Age									
Under 19 years	12.4	10.1	11.1	12.2	12.4	16.5	15.2	7.8	8.2
19 to 21 years	23.6	25.0	25.0	23.6	22.4	23.1	23.3	19.8	22.9
22 to 34 years	40.6	41.1	40.6	40.4	41.6	38.1	38.6	47.1	44.1
35 to 44 years	13.3	12.9	13.2	13.2	13.6	12.7	12.4	16.5	15.0
45 years and over	10.2	11.0	10.1	10.6	10.0	9.6	10.5	8.8	9.8
Race									
White	68.8	66.8	61.1	64.2	73.1	76.2	77.1	76.2	83.0
Black	28.6	30.3	35.4	33.1	24.5	22.1	20.9	22.9	13.1
Other	2.7	3.0	3.5	2.7	2.4	1.7	2.0	0.9	3.9

Education									
Less than 8 years	6.7	8.0	7.5	6.9	5.9	6.2	5.6	5.4	6.4
8 years	8.6	9.3	9.0	8.6	8.2	8.0	8.4	8.8	9.2
9 to 11 years	32.7	36.5	35.0	34.2	30.7	28.7	30.6	29.0	28.7
12 years	45.1	41.3	42.5	43.9	47.5	48.3	46.6	47.6	45.4
Over 12 years	7.0	4.9	6.0	6.4	7.7	8.8	8.8	9.2	10.3
Public assistance recipient									
Yes	4.2	5.7	5.3	5.2	2.9	2.7	2.7	3.0	1.3
No	95.8	94.3	94.7	94.8	97.1	97.3	97.3	97.0	98.7
Prior employment status									
Unemployed	65.3	65.9	72.4	66.7	60.2	62.8	66.3	67.3	65.1
Other	34.7	34.1	27.6	33.3	39.8	37.2	33.7	32.7	34.9

Source: Manpower Report of the President, 1971, Table F-7, p. 305.

determine whether or not a person is part of a family whose combined income and size place them below a poverty line.* Thus, despite the fact that MDTA has been explicitly concerned with raising incomes above poverty levels since at least 1966, judgments with respect to the effectiveness of MDTA training as an antipoverty device will have to be based on available characteristics other than family size and income.

Given this deficiency in the national data, we must draw conclusions about the nature of the enrollee population from characteristics related to poverty. The DOL defines a "disadvantaged" worker as one who lacks *suitable* employment and is either (1) a high school dropout, (2) a member of a minority group, (3) under 22 years of age, (4) 45 years of age or older, or (5) handicapped. Anyone receiving welfare payments is also considered disadvantaged. This broad definition is not very helpful since it is not directly related to poverty status. It is quite possible for a worker to fall within the DOL's definition of disadvantaged but still earn enough to bring his family above the poverty level. In addition, the available data do not even permit a determination of the number of "disadvantaged" trainees. The definition requires that at least two criteria—lack of suitable employment and an age or education criterion—be met simultaneously, yet the data report each separately. Thus it is impossible to know how many of the unemployed or underemployed also meet the other criteria. For example, we know that 81.4 percent of all MDTA institutional trainees were previously unemployed, but we do not know how many of these also constitute the 10.3 percent who are over 45 or the 12.2 percent who receive public assistance.

What conclusions can be drawn from the available national data? We can only state that it appears that many enrollees are not part of the "hardcore" group for which the programs are primarily designed. This is especially true for MDTA OJT programs where selection of enrollees was left to the discretion of employers. In this program 68.8 percent of enrollees have been white, a majority (52.1 percent) have completed high school, while only 6.7 percent have less than an elementary school education, and only 4 percent received public assistance. Institutional programs follow a similar but less extreme pattern. In this program over 60.4 percent of the enrolles have been white, 46.7 percent completed high school, while only 7.2 percent have less than an elementary school education. About one-third (32.0 percent) of the enrollees have been unemployed less than five weeks before entering training.

The data for the total enrollee population are somewhat distorted because they include the earlier years during which the program was not

---

*Data on the family income of MDTA enrollees have been gathered beginning in the year 1970. However, these income data are not cross-classified with family size, so it is impossible to determine poverty status from these figures. Because of this deficiency and because the data are not available for the years prior to 1970, we do not include these figures in our analysis.

explicitly concerned with serving the disadvantaged. The trend has been for increased enrollment from among this group. For example, the percentage of institutional trainees who were black increased from 21.4 percent in 1963 to 45.4 percent in 1968 and has dropped slightly since. Similarly, among OJT enrollees the percent who were black rose from 13.1 percent to 35.4 percent between 1963 and 1969. Based upon the available data, the fairest conclusion to be made is that many, probably a majority, of the enrollees in the MDTA programs, and particularly in MDTA OJT programs, have not been "disadvantaged." However, the proportion drawn from among the disadvantaged group increased during the program's history until its recent leveling off.

While the routinely reported data on MDTA programs do not include family size and income, some cross-tabulation figures on income and other variables are available from two studies of national samples of trainees enrolled in 1966[1] and in 1969.[2] Both studies use data from the Social Security Administration files to estimate the earnings of enrollees prior to training. As noted earlier, individuals' earnings are not an ideal measure of poverty status, but they can supplement the other available data. In both studies earnings were estimated only for trainees who were heads of households, a group constituting about two-thirds of all trainees. The 1966 study found that 50 percent of the OJT trainees and 80 percent of the institutional trainees had earnings below $3,000. The 1969 study found that 56 percent of the OJT trainees and 69 percent of the institutional trainees had earnings below the federal poverty line for a family of four. If allowance were made for the earnings of secondary workers in family income and for those trainees who are not family heads, the proportions would probably be reduced. Thus the studies support the finding that many trainees are not drawn from the target population but that institutional programs are more effective than OJT programs in this regard.

Enrollment in the JOBS program has been limited to those who fit the DOL's definition of disadvantaged. Therefore in this case it may be best to begin our inquiry by asking whether available training has been fully utilized rather than determining the proportion of trainees who are poor—that is, if training is limited to the disadvantaged and "creaming" does not occur, the critical question is whether administrators utilize all available training resources.

When President Johnson initiated the JOBS program in January 1968, the announced goal was 500,000 persons to be hired by June 1971. Initially, the program's achievements exceeded expectations. The program was administered by the National Alliance of Businessmen (NAB), which established local offices in the 50 largest U.S. cities. Over 40 percent of all firms contacted pledged to train disadvantaged workers. By July 1, 1969, over 338,000 jobs had been pledged.[3]

However, it soon became apparent that the businessmen's pledges were not a valid instrument for measuring the program's success. Pledges entailed no specification as to the date on which a trainee would be hired, the rate at which he would be paid, or the qualifications he would be required to possess. Many private firms that made pledges decided to meet their commitments without government subsidy or control. Consequently, there emerged two separate JOBS programs—one under goverment contract and one voluntary. However, totals provided by program administrators usually combine figures from both programs.

Data from the non-contract portion are scarce and unreliable. Non-contract employers almost always recruit and "certify" their trainees as disadvantaged themselves, rather than accept those who have been identified as meeting the DOL's definition of disadvantaged by the local employment service or community action agency. For example, in the New York City program, data made available by the DOL regional office covering the period up to November 30, 1969, indicate that only 2 percent of the contract program trainees were employer-certified whereas about 65 percent of the non-contract program trainees were employer-certified.[4] Data on the characteristics of non-contract employees are rarely reported to the DOL by employers, and we cannot reach any firm conclusion about the extent to which non-contract employers are making an additional effort to reach and train the disadvantaged. The best we can do is echo the cautious conclusion of another observer:

> The fact that most of the noncontract enrollees are employer-certified leaves the credibility of the non-contract aspects of the NAB-JOBS program in doubt. The requirement that a state employment service or CEP [Concentrated Employment Program] certify the employees hired under the Labor Department contracts conform to the criteria of "disadvantaged" lends those figures more weight, though some complain that anyone "with a black face and a torn shirt" can be certified. There has been no check of the validity of the claims of non-contract employers. Though they had little incentive for false reporting, the low percentages of reporting leave ample room for bias in the data. Considering the tight labor markets of 1968-69 as well as the locations of many of the firms involved, it is difficult to know whether the proportion of disadvantaged among non-contract hires exceeds that which would have occurred without the program.[5]

For the contract portion of the JOBS program we may return to our earlier question. Since all trainees are certified as disadvantaged by public agencies, we must ask to what extent available training positions are actually filled. Table 5.3 contains data on appropriations, obligations, and outlays

66

TABLE 5.3

Utilization of JOBS Program Funds

(millions of dollars)

Fiscal Year	Appropriation	Obligations	Outlays
1968	$104.7	$104.7	$ 4.2
1969	153.8	153.8	41.7
1970	300.0	148.8[a]	59.4[a]
1971	375.0	169.1	b

[a] As of March 31, 1970.

[b] Not available.

Source: Letter of April 15, 1970, from Malcolm Lovell, Jr., Deputy Assistant Secretary for manpower, U.S. Department of Labor, to Senate Subcommittee on Employment, Manpower, and Poverty, reprinted in U.S. Congress, Senate, Subcommittee on Employment, Manpower, and Poverty of the Committee on Labor and Public Welfare, *The JOBS Program: Background Information* (Washington, D.C., April 1970), pp. 110-11; and *Manpower Report of the President, 1972*, Table F-1, p. 261.

under the JOBS program. The figures indicate that the DOL has been unable to spend the sums appropriated for the program. The appropriation is the amount provided by Congress (at the administration's request) for the program. Obligations represent the value of contracts entered into with employers. Outlays are actual payments made under the contracts. Payments are based on the number of days a trainee remains with the company and are usually paid out every few weeks. Outlays will trail obligations since training may last up to 18 months and training under a contract may not begin until weeks or months after a contract has been signed. However, it is unlikely that these delays account for the entire difference between obligations and outlays. A substantial portion of the difference is undoubtedly accounted for by the failure of firms to hire and retain as many trainees as they had originally committed themselves to add to their work force. More significant is the recent (1970-71) gap between appropriations and obligations. Largely because of the general economic recession many corporations have been unable and unwilling to enter into agreements to hire new workers. Consequently the DOL has been unable to sign contracts for the full amount of its appropriations.

Further evidence that the private sector cannot fully utilize funds available to it is found in a study of the program in nine cities conducted by the Systems Development Corporation.[6] Data in Table 5.4 indicate that for the first series of contracts (MA-3) under the JOBS program only an average of 26 percent of the funds had been used despite the fact that 45 percent of the period covered by the contracts had elapsed. For subsequent (MA-4) contracts only 5 percent of the money had been spent while 15 percent of the period covered had passed. The authors of the study concluded,

> It is clear that the funds obligated under both MA-3 and MA-4 will not be utilized fully; with nearly half the contract performance period elapsed, MA-3 contractors have invoiced only slightly more than one-fourth of their available funds. The prospects that they can hire and retain enough trainees to catch up during the remaining year seem remote. MA-4 contractors, if anything, are even slower in making use of the money available to them.[7]

Additional, but less formal, evidence indicating that government is unable to spend, and business unable to use, all resources devoted to training the disadvantaged comes from journalistic sources. A *New York Times* correspondent, Paul Delaney, quoted administration officials at the end of 1970 as saying that the JOBS program was unable to secure commitments from private industry as extensive as they had anticipated. Delaney reported that "many local businessmen's alliances not only failed to obtain their job goals, but also were forced to cancel drives to seek more pledges and jobs."[8]

This examination of enrollment in federal training programs suggests two general conclusions. First, if training is made available to a broad segment of the population, as in the case of MDTA, some "creaming" will take place, and there will be difficulty in reaching the most disadvantaged. Second, if training is restricted to disadvantaged groups and requires the cooperation of the private sector, as in the case of the JOBS program, then fluctuations in the economy can adversely affect the viability of the program.

COMPLETING TRAINING

A second important issue to consider in assessing the impact of training programs is whether or not the poor successfully complete training. That is, once enrolled in training do the poor complete the program and acquire the skills that training is intended to provide them? If, once they are enrolled, the poor do not remain and "graduate" from the training program, logic would indicate that the effectiveness of the service is limited.

The national data (Table 5.5) indicate that approximately two-thirds of all enrollees in MDTA programs complete their training, with the figure being

TABLE 5.4

Performance of JOBS Program Contractors

City	MA-3 Contractors			MA-4 Contractors		
	Number of Contracts Reviewed	Contract Funds	Percent of Funds Invoiced*	Number of Contracts Reviewed	Contract Funds	Percent of Funds Invoiced*
Chicago	32	$5,595,253	29	13	$3,101,904	2
Kansas City	8	1,436,307	23	20	2,231,478	9
Los Angeles	31	5,219,553	25	30	7,626,756	3
Minneapolis	12	1,304,010	15	1	48,868	13
New Orleans	6	1,151,986	28	7	1,149,842	**
Pittsburgh	13	1,970,854	35	8	1,141,048	6
San Antonio	15	1,175,027	18	10	619,213	7
Seattle	6	1,125,078	29	2	54,371	**
Tampa	2	287,188	20	12	1,327,318	12
Total	125	$19,265,256	26	103	$17,300,198	5

*As of May, 1969. Contract time elapsed averaged 45 percent of the total performance period for MA-3 contracts and 15 percent for MA-4 contracts.

**Less than one half of one percent.

Source: Systems Development Corporation, "Evaluation of the JOBS Program in Nine Cities" (Falls Church, Va.: the Corporation, September 1969), pp. 18-19.

TABLE 5.5

Enrollments and Completions in MDTA Programs, Fiscal Years 1963-71
(thousands of people)

	Total	1971	1970	1969	1968	1967	1966	1965	1964	1963
Institutional										
Enrolled	1,134.0	155.6	130.0	135.0	140.0	150.0	177.5	145.3	68.6	32.0
Completed	742.0	90.3	85.0	95.0	91.0	109.0	117.7	88.8	46.0	19.2
OJT										
Enrolled	473.0	*	91.0	85.0	101.0	115.0	58.3	11.6	9.0	2.1
Completed	335.5	*	62.0	65.0	73.2	83.6	38.0	7.5	5.3	0.9
Total										
Enrolled	1,607.0	155.6	221.0	220.0	241.0	265.0	235.8	156.9	77.6	34.1
Completed	1,075.5	90.3	147.0	160.0	164.2	192.6	155.7	96.3	51.3	20.1

*The OJT program was ended in 1971.

Source: Manpower Report of the President, U.S. Department of Labor (Washington, D.C. annual).

somewhat higher for OJT than for institutional training. The figures are only approximate because the number graduating cannot be related directly to the number enrolled for the same year. For example, some people completing training in fiscal 1969 may have enrolled in fiscal 1968 and many enrolling in fiscal 1969 will not graduate until fiscal 1970. In any given time period the enrollee population is not the same as the population of dropouts and completers combined.

There is no direct way to determine how many of the graduates are drawn from the disadvantaged population or if the poor are represented among the graduates in the same proportion as they are among the total enrollee population. We estimated earlier that approximately half the enrollees are likely to be "poor." If we add to this the fact that two-thirds of all enrollees complete training, then the proportion of poor trainees who graduate can fall between one-third and the entire number. To obtain a more precise estimate of the degree to which training is successfully undertaken by the poor, it is necessary to examine additional data.

The existing relevant national data report the characteristics of dropouts and completers for the fiscal years 1968 and 1969 (Table 5.6). It is important to note that the data do not report family income (or poverty status), but only characteristics related to poverty. As in the discussion of enrollment, we can deal only with variables related to poverty status.

The data in Table 5.6 permit only a few limited conclusions about the rates of completion for those most likely to be poor. Overall, race appears to make little difference in the probablity of a person's completing training. Of the total group in 1969, whites constituted 56 percent of the dropouts and 58 percent of the completers, while nonwhites constituted 44 percent and 42 percent, respectively. For 1968, the figures for whites were 53 percent and 53 percent and for blacks 47 percent and 47 percent. However, when disaggregated by race and sex the figures show that black and while females have similar rates of completion; white males are somewhat more likely to complete than black males. Education appears to exert some influence on completion, for the better-educated are overrepresented among completers, but the differences are slight.

A more detailed analysis of the characteristics of 406 trainees enrolled in four different courses in four different communities in Michigan was performed by a research group at Michigan State University under contract for the Department of Labor. The group's data parallel the findings outlined above. The personal characteristics used to define the disadvantaged population had little bearing on the probability of completing training. In a summary section the Michigan group states,

> Those hypotheses specifically suggesting varied training outcome as a result of differing social and social-psychological attributes of the trainees must be rejected. Training seems to be successfully under-taken by all types of persons who are properly motivated. Such

71

TABLE 5.6

Characteristics of Trainees Who Dropped Out and Who Completed Training in MDTA Institutional Projects
(percent distribution)

| | Fiscal 1969 | | | | | | Fiscal 1968 | | | | | |
| | Total | | Male | | Female | | Total | | Male | | Female | |
	DO[a]	C[b]	DO	C	DO	C	DO	C	DO	C	DO	C
Race												
White	56	58	58	66	51	50	53	53	55	57	49	49
Nonwhite	44	42	42	34	49	50	47	47	45	43	51	51
Total	100	100	100	100	100	100	100	100	100	100	100	100
Education												
Less than 8	9	7	11	10	5	4	8	8	10	11	5	5
8th grade	10	9	12	12	6	6	11	9	14	12	7	7
9 to 11th grade	43	35	46	37	40	33	48	37	49	40	44	34
12th grade	35	42	29	37	46	47	30	39	25	33	39	45
Over 12th grade	3	7	2	4	4	9	3	7	2	4	5	10
Total	100	100	100	100	100	100	100	100	100	100	100	100

[a]Dropouts.

[b]Completers.

Source: *Education and Training*, Eighth Annual Report of the U.S. Department of Health, Education, and Welfare to the Congress on Training Activities Under the MDTA, April 1970 (Washington, D.C., 1970), Table D-1, p.76.

differences, based on age or education, for example, which one might assume are significant, derived from the logic of the labor market, become open to question as a result of our research.[9]

These two studies suggest that the poor are as likely to complete training as are the nonpoor. Using their findings, we can estimate that approximately two-thirds of each group of enrollees graduate from the MDTA programs.

For OJT, particularly in the JOBS program, it is more difficult to analyze the probability of successful completion of training among the poor. In the contract portion of the JOBS program all trainees are certified as disadvantaged, so it is the experience of the total enrollee population that is relevant. However, records of completion are not kept. Training consists of work experience supplemented by basic education coupled with other social services that the employer ordinarily would not provide but that the government has contracted to subsidize. Completion of training means staying on the job for the period of time for which the government has agreed to subsidize the ancillary services. Since the government reimburses firms on a per diem basis, the available data refer to the number of days an employee remains with the firm. Hence duration of employment is the significant variable.

Table 5.7 provides data on the number of individuals hired and the number remaining employed under the contract portion of the JOBS program. MA-3 contracts refer to those contracts between the government and private employers written between March 1968 and August 1968. The maximum period for which a firm could receive payments under these contracts was two years, but the average duration was eight months. There were 45,300 people hired under MA-3 contracts, of whom 14,564 (32.2 percent) were still working on the job on January 31, 1970. Some of those no longer on the job may have completed training and moved on to better jobs, but the Department of Labor has reported that 93 percent of those no longer on the job left before completing eight months of work. Thus most of those hired under MA-3 contracts and not working as of January 31, 1970, are probably individuals who did not complete their training cycle. The MA-4 contracts, written between September 1968 and May 1969, provided for a maximum of 18 months and many contracts were probably still in effect in January 1970. Consequently, the actual retention rate will probably be lower than that indicated in the table. MA-5 contracts were still being written in January 1971. Of the available data, the experience with MA-3 contracts appears to be the most valid indicator of retention in the JOBS program. From this experience it can be estimated that only one in three trainees completes the training period.

In summary the available evidence on the completion of training among individuals at or near the poverty level who enroll in training programs suggests the following conclusions:

TABLE 5.7

Status of Trainees Under JOBS Program
Contracts as of January 31, 1970

Contracts	Number Hired	Number Still Employed	Retention Rate (percent)
MA-3	45,300	14,564	32.2
MA-4	31,368	14,348	45.7
MA-5	7,898	{5,566}	{69.3}
All other	137		
Total	84,703	34,478	40.7

Source: U.S. Senate, Subcommittee on Employment, Manpower, and Poverty of the Committee on Labor and Public Welfare, *The JOBS Program: Background Information,* Committee Report (Washington, D.C., 1970), pp. 114-120.

(1) In MDTA institutional programs where training is not restricted to the poor, those who possess characteristics associated with poverty status experience approximately the same rates of success as do other trainees—about 70 percent.

(2) In the JOBS program, which provides OJT opportunities for the disadvantaged only, about 35 percent of those hired complete their training.

The strikingly different figures indicate a great variability in the effectiveness of training programs and suggest that the JOBS program, which depends on private-sector initiative and cooperation, is vulnerable to shifts in the business cycle.

INCOME GAINS FROM TRAINING

The final factor that an evaluation of training as an antipoverty program must consider is the extent to which training raises the earnings of lower-income trainees.

The only large-scale survey of MDTA trainees that used a control group was undertaken by the National Opinion Research Center (NORC) for the U.S. Department of Labor in 1966. The composition of the control group

74

was determined by asking trainees to give the name of a friend or neighbor of the same sex who was unemployed at about the same time as the trainee. The regression analysis of the NORC data found that MDTA training had no effect on wages. "MDTA training had no effect on hourly wages for those who found full-time employment after training."[10] However, MDTA completers were found to have made greater gains in total income than the controls. The net effect of completing training was a gain of $10.08 in weekly income. How can training increase family income without raising wage rates? The author of the study, Earl Main, suggested the following explanation; "The probable answer lies in the fact that more completers than controls were employed when interviewed (78% versus 55%, with dropouts in between at 65%). Because more trainees had jobs, trainees had a higher average family income than nontrainees. The logical conclusion is that MDTA training increased incomes by helping obtain steadier employment rather than higher wages."[11]

It is not certain if the income differences attributable to greater employment stability rather than higher wages are the result of training. The differences may be a function of differential selection in the determination of the control group. MDTA completers may be more highly motivated or differ in some other crucial variable not included in the regression analysis. Main summarized the problem as follows:

> The major unresolved question is how much of the estimated net effect of training is really due to some other variable not included in the analysis. An attempt was made to include all available information which might contribute to the explanation of employment differences, but most of the variables included are demographic. It is probable that motivation, intelligence, or other factors have some contribution to make. Those who want jobs the most and who have the best minds might be most likely to find employment and to use every means available to obtain employment, including MDTA job training courses. Therefore, the true effect of training on employment may well be smaller than the estimates given in the report.[12]

David Farber of the U.S. Bureau of the Budget has used data from the Social Security Administration's Continuous Work History Sample (CWHS) to examine the impact of training on earnings.[13] He compared the quarterly earnings of a group of MDTA trainees before and after training with similar data for all workers in the CWHS having the same age, sex, and race characteristics. The Farber comparisons revealed that for nearly every group of institutional trainees the trainees earned less than the controls before training and this *gap widened* after training. For OJT programs the results were mixed, with some groups narrowing the difference between controls and trainees. The implication of Farber's data is that MDTA programs generally do not raise the earnings of trainees beyond the gains that normally occur over time.

Herman Miller has criticized Farber's approach because he feels the control group is an inappropriate one. Miller argues that standardizing only for age, race, and sex does not assure that the two groups are comparable. The control group is a representative sample of all workers and includes individuals whose educational achievement and career prospects are likely to be more favorable than those of MDTA trainees who are selected because of their special labor market disadvantages. Moreover, "Mr. Farber's system assumes that all of these differences as well as many others relating to mental health, emotional stability, and related factors can be largely eliminated by use of a standardization procedure. This seems like a very heroic assumption."[14]

Because of the difficulty in selecting an appropriate control group, other surveys have been limited to before and after comparisons of trainees' earnings. The before and after comparisons are useful because they permit disaggregation of the trainee population into groups having different earnings levels prior to training. Cross-classifications of a sample of over 21,000 MDTA institutional trainees prepared by the Department of Health, Education, and Welfare found that over 70 percent of the employed graduates had their hourly earnings raised, and the figure was higher for those with the lowest pretraining earnings (See Table 5.8).

TABLE 5.8

**Pretraining and Posttraining Earnings of
Sample of MDTA Institutional Graduates***

Pretraining Earnings	Number of Graduates	Percent Earning Same or Less	Percent Earning More
Less than $1.25	3,981	11	89
$1.25-$1.49	4,830	14	86
$1.50-$1.74	3,964	25	75
$1.75-$1.99	1,976	31	69
$2.00-$2.24	1,999	36	64
$2.25-$2.49	1,046	43	57
$2.50-$2.99	1,739	64	36
$3.00 and over	1,501	100	-
Total	21,036	31	69

*Sample includes graduates in fiscal year 1968 with earnings reported both before and after training.

Source: Data reported in *Education and Training: Doorway to the Seventies,* U.S. Department of Health, Education, and Welfare (Washington, D.C., 1970).

Levitan and Mangum used Social Security data to analyze the anti-poverty impact of MDTA training (See Table 5.9). They found that of those completing training, over 60 percent increased their earnings. The percentage was highest for family heads with below-poverty incomes and was almost as high for nonfamily heads but was relatively low for nonpoor family heads. The figures from before and after comparisons indicate that training is effective for those poor who complete the programs.

TABLE 5.9

Changes in Earnings of MDTA
Institutional Graduates*

Pretraining Status of Graduate	Percent with Increased Earnings	Percent Earning Same or Less
Total	64	36
Family heads earnings under $3,000	70	30
Family heads earning above $3,000	28	72
Nonfamily heads	71	29

*Refers to graduates enrolled in 1965 who reported earnings both before and after training.

Source: OASDHI [Old Age, Survivors, Disability and Health Insurance] data reported in Sar Levitan and Garth Mangum, *Federal Training and Work Programs in the Sixties* (Ann Arbor, Mich.: Institute of Labor and Industrial Relations, 1969).

SUMMARY

This chapter has relied on data from a variety of sources to analyze the antipoverty impact of training programs. In terms of the three basic criteria set forth in the preceding chapter, the findings may be summarized as follows:

(1) Judged on the basis of "vertical efficiency," training programs have had only limited success in reaching the target population (the poor). Such individuals represent about half of all trainees in institutional training programs but a smaller fraction of the OJT trainees. In the JOBS program, which is restricted to the disadvantaged, all available resources have not been used because cooperating employers were unable to offer the anticipated level of training opportunities.

(2) Those poor individuals who enter training appear to have an equal probability of successfully completing training compared to other trainees. The programs are relatively successful in their holding power, with only about one-third of all trainees (poor and nonpoor) not completing training.

(3) Before- and after-training comparisons in two large-scale studies indicate that training programs have increased the incomes of completers, and particularly the incomes of previously low-wage trainees. However, both these studies included only completers who found jobs, and both failed to use a control group to determine if other factors might explain the income gains. One study utilizing a control group and incorporating the experiences of all types of completers found no significant change in wage rates but a slight gain in the amount of employment secured by completers. A second study using a control group found training generally had an unfavorable impact on earnings, but the selection of this control group is subject to serious criticism. Thus the evidence is inconclusive but does indicate that whatever gains might result from training are greatest among low-income enrollees.

NOTES

1. Sar Levitan and Garth Mangum, *Federal Training and Work Programs in the Sixties* (Ann Arbor, Mich.: Institute for Labor and Industrial Relations, 1969), pp. 40ff.

2. Decision Making Information, "MDTA Outcomes Study, Final Report" (Santa Ana, Cal., 1971); the findings of this study are presented as summarized in Garth Mangum and John Walsh, *A Decade of Manpower Development and Training* (Salt Lake City: Olympus, 1973), chapter 2.

3. Sar Levitan, Garth Mangum, and Robert Taggart, *Economic Opportunity in the Ghetto: The Partnership of Government and Business* (Baltimore: The Johns Hopkins Press, 1970), p. 20.

4. Data for the New York City JOBS program is unpublished data furnished to the author by Harry Barletta, the New York regional representative of the Office of Manpower Management Data System, Manpower Administration, U.S. Department of Labor.

5. Levitan, Mangum, and Taggart, *Economic Opportunity in the Ghetto*, pp. 22-23.

6. Systems Development Corporation, "Evaluation of the JOBS Program in Nine Cities" (Falls Church, Va.: the Corporation, September 1969).

7. *Ibid.*, p. 17.

8. *The New York Times,* January 26, 1970, p. 1.

9. Sigmund Nosow, *Retraining Under MDTA: A Study of Attributes of Trainees Associated with Successful Retraining* (East Lansing: School of Labor and Industrial Relations, Michigan State University, January 1968), p. III-3.

10. Earl Main, "A Nationwide Evaluation of MDTA Institutional Job Training," *Journal of Human Resources* 3, 2 (Spring 1968).

11. *Ibid.*, pp. 165-66.

12. *Ibid.*, p. 169.

13. Farber's work has not been published, but Herman Miller has reviewed Farber's calculations and prepared a paper on the subject. Herman Miller, "Critique of David Farber's Methods of Evaluating the Gains in Earnings of MDTA Trainees" (Washington, D.C.: National Manpower Policy Task Force, Xerox, September 1972). This description of Farber's findings is based on Miller's paper.

14. Miller, "Critique of David Farber's Methods," p. 12.

6

THE IMPACT
OF COMMUNITY ACTION
AND THE POLITICAL STRATEGY

In Chapter 3 it was asserted that the enactment of Title II of the Economic Opportunity Act, the Community Action Program, represented an opportunity for federal antipoverty intervention to follow the political strategy. In this chapter the relationship between the CAP and the political strategy will be analyzed in greater detail, and an effort will be made to evaluate the effectiveness of the political strategy by examining the experience under the CAP in the context of the community power-structure dimensions elaborated in Chapter 4. Specifically, this chapter's three sections will (1) examine the extent to which local community action agencies (CAAs) pursued the political strategy; (2) review and analyze published case studies of local CAAs to see if they provide data relating to changes in community decision-making patterns; and (3) analyze data from unpublished reports contracted for by the OEO to evaluate the impact of CAAs on local decision-making.

MAXIMUM FEASIBLE PARTICIPATION
AND THE POLITICAL STRATEGY

The provision of Title II of the EOA that became best known and that frequently is identified with the political strategy is Section 202(a)(3). This section stipulated that a community action program must be one that is "developed, conducted, and administered with the maximum feasible participation of residents of the areas and members of the groups served." In fact it was argued in Chapter 3 that inclusion of this provision was evidence of the intentions of many of the drafters of the legislation to make possible implementation of the political strategy through the CAP.

When the CAP became operative no precise definition was given to the "maximum feasible participation" clause. That a CAA was supposed to develop an organizational base for expanding the influence of a city's poorer residents was clear in the *CAP Guide* issued by the OEO for the use of applicants seeking funds under the program. The *Guide* stated,

> Achievement of meaningful participation shall be a continuing objective of every Community Action Program, since it is through their own effective participation that the residents and groups to be served can most readily achieve the objective of a permanent increase in their capacity to deal with their own problems without further assistance.[1]

But the OEO officials were not precise in defining the nature of "meaningful" or "maximum" participation and in clarifying the relative importance of the political strategy. As a consequence "maximum feasible participation" took on three meanings. First, it was associated with the political strategy; a CAP's mission was to organize the poor. Second, it was identified with having representatives of the poor serve on the governing boards of the CAPs. Finally, it was associated with the employment of local residents in the CAP. In particular, the poor were to be employed in the provision of social services in new paraprofessional roles.[2]

It should be noted that the three objectives are not mutually exclusive nor are they integrally connected. A CAA might seek to organize the poor (political strategy), but its board might not be composed primarily of representatives of the client population and it might employ outside professionals. Alternatively, a CAA might be governed by a board composed in the majority of spokesmen of the impoverished, but they could choose to provide traditional social services and give little attention to political organization. The traditional social services might (or might not) be provided by professionals (or paraprofessionals).

Each of the approaches to maximum feasible participation was pursued in varying degrees. Employment of indigenous personnel was widespread. An early (1966) study by a private consulting firm, Daniel Yankelovich, Inc., found that the CAAs in nine large cities had hired considerable numbers of local poor to perform essential tasks. More than 5,000 nonprofessionals had been employed in the nine cities; 79 percent of this group were black, and 62 percent had been unemployed prior to their present job.[3] The study concluded that the new careers approach in the CAP was widely and successfully implemented:

Our overall conclusion is that the program is now operationally viable: a large number of previously unemployed or under-employed poor people without background or training for the kind of work they are now doing have been routinely hired, have received some training, and are working hard and enthusiastically on their jobs. After some months of experience, supervising professional and agency personnel in the CAA's feel that the non-professionals are filling an indispensable role rather well.[4]

Representation of the poor on governing boards was more problematical. EOA Section 202(a)(4) specified only that a CAP be a program "which is conducted, administered or coordinated by a public or private nonprofit agency (other than a political party), or a combination thereof." There were originally no statutory requirements regarding the composition of a CAA's governing board. The first Director of Community Action Programs for OEO, Jack Conway, often used an analogy of a three-legged stool to describe the composition of an ideal CAA. The three legs were municipal officials, representatives of established social welfare agencies, and representatives of the poor. The initial *CAP Guide* was vague, specifying little more than that a CAA "must provide ample opportunity for partici-pation in policy making by the major public and private agencies responsible for services and programs concerned with poverty, other elements of the community as a whole, and the population to be served by the Community Action Program."[5] The result was a variety of arrangements incorporating different standards for representation on the boards. At the end of the CAP's first year of operation OEO reported that 27 percent of the representatives on local boards were representatives of the poor and at the end of the second year the figure was 30 percent.[6] However, these averages obscure the range, which included boards with no representation for the poor to those where the poor had a majority.

The 1966 amendments to the EOA required that at least one-third of the members of the governing boards of CAAs represent the poor. The 1967 Greene amendment, named after its prime sponsor, Congresswoman Edith Greene, stipulated that appropriate local governments could assume sponsor-ship of CAPs, but even then at least one-third of the members of the governing board must represent the poor.*

---

*The Greene amendment was also know as the "bosses and boll weevil" amendment because it was supported strongly by many Southern politicians, who objected to the activities of community action groups like the Child Development Group of Mississippi, and by big-city mayors, who wanted the CAAs to be under local municipal agencies for patronage and other reasons. As a result of the mayors' efforts—notably those of Chicago's Richard Daley, New York's Robert Wagner, Los Angeles's Sam Yorty, and Philadelphia's James Tate—the U.S. Conference of Mayors urged municipal control of CAAs at its 1965 meeting, and the testimony of these mayors before Congress helped secure passage of the Greene amendment.

A study to assess the significance of this amendment was required by Congress and conducted for OEO by Daniel Yankelovich, Inc.[7] The study examined changes in the sponsorship and composition of governing boards in 53 localities in 37 states during the year after the passage of the Greene amendment. The three-volume study concluded that the Greene amendment had little affect on CAA governing boards. In only three cases was the CAA changed from a private to a public agency. However, among the 50 agencies whose status had not been altered, significant changes in the composition of the governing board occurred in 23. In most instances, the change was an increase in the number (and proportion) of representatives from public agencies (municipal government) and a corresponding reduction in the number (and proportion) of members from the nonprofit social service agencies, with little change in the role of the poor.

The issue of representation of the poor on CAA governing boards raises important issues relating to the nature of representation. Who speaks for the poor? Must a representative of the poor be poor himself? Paul Petersen has studied representation of the poor in the CAP.[8] Petersen distinguished among three types of representation: descriptive representation, formal representation, and substantive representation. Descriptive representation refers to "the extent to which the representatives reflect accurately the characteristics of those who they formally represent."[9] Formal representation is based on the arrangements that determine the way in which a representative is selected. For example, a constituency is represented by a person whom it elects. Substantive representation is based upon the actions of the representative.

Using these concepts Petersen examined the nature of representation of the poor in the CAA of each of three cities: New York, Philadelphia, and Chicago. He found that descriptive representation was not a significant issue. Few representatives had socioeconomic characteristics similar to their constituents, although Philadelphia, with 40 percent of its poverty council members with annual incomes below $6,000, did meet the criterion of descriptive representation. He concluded,

> Socially descriptive representation was far less controversial in these three cities than were the arrangements for formal representation. Neighborhood groups were far less insistent that any income limit be placed upon those chosen to represent the residents of low income communities. Their reticence on this point may have been due to the tendency for organizations to recruit the more skilled, better educated, and more affluent members of the community; many of their leaders would be disqualified from participating if a strict income limit were placed on those who could serve as representatives of the poor. The extent to which socially descriptive representation was implemented must be

83

attributed to OEO's dogged insistence that at least some of those representing the poor come from similar backgrounds themselves.[10]

With respect to formal and substantive representation, Petersen found the following patterns: Chicago had limited formal representation (CAP members appointed by the mayor) and limited substantive representation; Philadelphia had high formal representation (direct election of poverty council members) but only moderate substantive representation; New York had moderate formal representation (appointments via neighborhood organizations), but its substantive representation was high, leading to extensive political conflicts.

Petersen's research does not yield a definitive answer to the problems of representation, but it provides evidence of the different patterns of representation that characterized the selection and composition of CAA governing boards.

The extent to which the maximum feasible participation clause, and the CAP in general, was implemented through the adoption of a political strategy is another complex issue. Four surveys of CAAs bear on this question. Kenneth Clark and Jeannette Hopkins surveyed 51 CAAs in 27 states in all regions of the nation.[11] They then divided the components of each CAA's program into three categories: services, community organization, and community action. The 51 CAAs were found to have 406 identifiable program components or elements. The distribution of these program elements is presented in Table 6.1. Most of the programs were devoted to the provision of services, and only a relatively small number sought to organize the poor. The authors concluded, "The major findings of the tabulation was that, despite the designation of *community action,* programs seem to be functioning primarily in terms of *services.*"[12]

A similar conclusion was reached by a study undertaken for the Subcommittee on Employment, Manpower, and Poverty of the Senate Committee on Labor and Public Welfare. Consultants analyzed CAPs in 35 communities across the nation. The study's findings are summarized as follows:

> A review of the 35 case studies reveals that the Community Action Program in its dominant form is a new kind of service program, with services directed primarily to individuals rather than to families or other groups . . . .
>
> Conversely, except for a very small number of communities the Community Action Program does not involve a predominant commitment to the strategy of giving power to the poor, of deliberate confrontation with established powers, of purposefully created conflict. This is a stereotype placed on CAP in its early days by a few articulate advocates of this approach and echoed

ever since by journalists, who have not examined what is actually going on. Yet, this approach is found only in San Francisco, Syracuse, and Newark of the 35 communities studied. All three were included in the sample because of the controversy surrounding them, but this writer does not know of any other community where this approach predominates.[13]

TABLE 6.1

**Elements of Community Action Programs
in 51 Cities**

Program Element	Number	Percent
Services	*317*	*78.1*
Educational	116	28.6
Social services	103	25.4
Job training	52	12.8
Health services	23	5.7
Housing	10	2.5
Legal services and delinquency	13	3.2
Community organization	*34*	*8.4*
Organization for program involvement	15	3.7
Organization in neighborhood centers	12	3.0
Settlement house organization	7	1.7
Other community action	*55*	*13.5*
Use of indigenous staff	23	5.7
Use of indigenous community groups	12	3.0
Training of local leaders	10	2.5
All other	10	2.5
Total	406	100.0

Source: Kenneth Clark and Jeanette Hopkins, *A Relevant War Against Poverty,* (New York: Harper & Row, 1969), pp. 64-65.

A study of CAAs in 20 cities in three regions of the United States (Northeast, border, and Southwest) confirmed the Clark-Hopkins finding. The author, Stephen Rose of Brandeis University, examined the program elements and budgets of the CAAs in each city.[14] He identified 350 different program elements in the 20 agencies. Only 11 of these programs (3

85

percent) could be identified as exclusively following the political strategy. However, there was considerable variation among the cities. Over half the cities had no programs or funds devoted to the political strategy; while one city spent 28 percent of its budget on political programs, the others ranged from 1.8 percent to 17.8 percent. Rose attached greatest significance to the 3 percent figure and concluded that the Community Action Program had been transformed into a traditional service program.

James Sundquist's study of 27 communities in eight states led to somewhat contradictory conclusions.[15] His focus was on coordination in the delivery of local services, and he found CAAs did not function well in this respect because they were frequently viewed as the "local militants" by other agencies. Sundquist presented his finding as follows:

> But the CAA's also were engaged, in one way or another in most localities in organizing the poor as a political force to carry on the assault on the status quo under their power and in their own name. This added a new and immensely significant dimension to the conflict that community action had engendered within communities—the dimension, above all others, that has made community action "controversial." The amount of emphasis that CAA's and their neighborhood centers gave to organizing the poor for political action—as distinct from providing services to them—is difficult to measure quantitatively. One OEO sponsored study concluded that with few exceptions the neighborhood centers had not attempted to organize the poor. However, in terms of the CAAs' image . . . they were seen in their communities as putting great emphasis on organizing the poor.[16]

A fifth study, of much smaller scale, should also be noted. Peter Eisinger, as part of his doctoral dissertation, examined the activities of five community action groups (CAGs) in Brooklyn. By reviewing the newsletters published by these agencies he was able to divide the reported activities into "political" and "service" categories (see Table 6.2). His conclusion: "The most important observation to make is that *all* the CAGs do behave as political forces to some extent. Thus the unqualified answer to the question, Does the CAG indeed act as a political force? is affirmative."[17]

National expenditure data from OEO on the CAP provide additional evidence with which to assess the extent to which CAAs implemented the political strategy. While initially all CAP funds could be spent in accord with the plans of the local CAA, Congress soon began to "earmark" funds. The earmarking of funds was to ensure support for "national-emphasis" programs that were essentially service-provision programs. Examples of these national-emphasis programs include Head Start, a program of educational and health services for preschool children, and the neighborhood health centers program. Table 6.3 contains data showing the amounts and proportions of

TABLE 6.2

**Activities of Brooklyn Community
Action Groups by Type
(percent distribution)**

CAG	Political Activity	Service Activity	Other Activity
Brownsville	54.5	21.2	24.3
Williamsburg	51.4	40.2	8.6
Fort Greene	47.6	45.2	7.2
South Brooklyn	47.3	47.3	5.4
East New York	41.1	53.0	6.0
Youth-in-Action	23.4	68.0	8.6

Source: Peter Eisinger, "The Anti-Poverty Community Action Group as a Political Force in the Ghetto" (unpublished Ph.D. dissertation, Political Science Department, Yale University, 1969), p. 113.

CAP funds for local initiative programs and for national-emphasis programs in fiscal years 1965, 1968, and 1971. One way to interpret these figures is that funds available for local initiative programs represent the maximum level of resources available for the political strategy, since national-emphasis programs are primarily service programs. The table shows that the proportion of CAP funds available for local initiative programs declined from 48.7 percent in 1965 to 37.3 percent in 1968 to 21.0 percent in 1971. Thus a smaller share of resources were available for implementing the political strategy, and increasing importance has been assigned to the provision of services. However, it is important to note that considerable sums (over $300 million annually) are still being spent for local initiative programs, and it is still possible for local CAAs to receive support for implementing a political strategy. In fact, the absolute amount of money available for local initiative programs has risen, although it has not kept pace with total CAP money.

It should be noted that an interpretation of the budget data in Table 6.3, which allocates all national-emphasis program money to the service strategy, is subject to a wide margin of error. Many programs funded with national-emphasis or "earmarked" money have been channeled into activities that can be considered part of a political strategy. Consider, for example, the case of the Martin Luther King, Jr., Neighborhood Health Center in the South Bronx section of New York City. Although funded as part of the

OEO health services program, it has engaged in political activities along with supplying medical services. The center has a Community Health Advocacy Department, which views its role this way: "Effective advocacy in a disadvantaged area requires more than the pressing of claims and the winning of cases: it requires efforts to build up the supply and the effectiveness of the community's resources."[18] The legal services program also provides examples of ostensibly service programs that are pursuing political activities,[19] and the Head Start program, which is intended primarily to provide early childhood education, funded a project in Mississippi, the Child Development Group of Mississippi, which actively sought to organize rural blacks. Thus it is difficult to gauge the total funds deployed on behalf of the political strategy, and the use of local initiative funds alone may lead to serious underestimation of the support for the political strategy.

TABLE 6.3

Allocation of National CAP Funds

(millions of dollars)

	Fiscal 1965		Fiscal 1968		Fiscal 1971	
	Amount	Percent	Amount	Percent	Amount	Percent
Local initiative programs	$115.2	48.7	$323.3	37.3	$328.9	21.0
National-emphasis programs	121.3	41.3	543.5	62.7	1234.0	79.0
Head Start	96.4	40.8	321.2	37.1	578.0	37.0
Follow Through	-	-	14.6	1.7	90.0	5.8
Emergency food and medicine	-	-	12.8	1.5	175.0	11.1
Health services	-	-	33.2	3.8	160.0	10.2
Legal services	-	-	35.9	4.1	90.0	5.8
Family planning	-	-	9.0	1.0	30.0	1.9
Senior citizens	-	-	2.5	.3	12.0	.8
All other	24.9	10.5	114.3	13.1	99.0	6.3
Total: CAP	$236.5	100.0	$866.8	100.0	$1562.9	100.0

Source: Adapted from Sar Levitan, *The Great Society's Poor Law: A New Approach to Poverty* (Baltimore: The Johns Hopkins Press, 1969), Table 3-3, p. 123; and Congressional Quarterly Inc., *CQ Almanac, 1969* (Washington, D.C., 1970).

Our review indicates that no broadly applicable generalization can be made about the extent to which the more than 1,000 CAAs across the nation have sought to follow a political strategy. Many by inclination, and others by congressional mandate, are involved primarily in the provision of more or less traditional social services. But to varying degrees, many, and perhaps most, CAAs have sought to organize and politicise their constituents.

EVALUATION OF THE POLITICAL STRATEGY

The previous section pointed out that CAAs funded under Title II of the EOA did, in varying degrees, follow a political strategy. The remaining problem is the evaluation of the effectiveness of this strategy in achieving its goals. As outlined in Chapter 4, the goals of this strategy are to (1) enchance the political resources of the poor in the local community decision-making processes, (2) widen the scope of activities or issues in which poor citizens participate, and (3) bring forward subjects previously regarded as "nonissues" for public consideration. As a first step we shall analyze the published studies of the CAP in the context of these criteria.

Perhaps the best-known evaluative work is Daniel Moynihan's *Maximum Feasible Misunderstanding*. After reviewing the philosophical and legislative origins of the CAP, Moynihan provides a capsule history of the activities of two community action agencies: Mobilization For Youth (MFY) a pre-EOA agency that was subsequently funded by the OEO, and the Crusade for Opportunity, a Syracuse OEO agency. Both these organizations devoted a considerable portion of their efforts and resources to the political strategy. Moynihan summarizes the impact of their efforts as follows:

> Seemingly it comes to this. Over and over again, the attempt by official and quasi-official agencies (such as the Ford Foundation) to organize poor communities led first to the radicalization of the middle-class persons who began the effort; next to a certain amount of stirring among the poor, but accompanied by heightened racial antagonism on the part of the poor if they happen to be black; next to the retaliation from the larger white community; whereupon it would emerge that the Community Action Agency, which had talked so much, been so much in the headlines, promised so much in the way of change in the fundamentals of things, was powerless. A creature of a Washington bureaucracy, subject to discontinuation without notice. Finally, much bitterness all around.[20]

The thrust of Moynihan's argument is that the CAP had no substantive effect and served only to arouse antagonism and bitterness. In terms of the criteria suggested for evaluating the CAP, Moynihan's work indicates that there was no change in any of the three criteria as a result of the CAP. Whatever new resources groups representing the poor received as a result of the CAP were quickly withdrawn when the groups began to use them for political ends. The militant CAAs were, therefore, unable to broaden the scope of their participation or develop new issues.

There are two important reasons why Moynihan's work cannot serve as a basis for generalization about the impact of the CAP. The first shortcoming of Moynihan's evaluation is that he restricted himself to two cases that represent one end of a continuum in the degree of emphasis attached to the political strategy by CAAs. Although the theme of Moynihan's writing, as evidenced in the title of his book and a key chapter ("Community Action Loses") as well as the above passage, is that the entire CAP was a failure, a cautious reader can find evidence that Moynihan intended the generalization to apply only to the most militant CAAs. Examine the following summary paragraph:

> At the risk of oversimplification, it might be said that the CAP's most closely controlled by City Hall were disappointing, and that the ones most antagonistic were destroyed. *There was a large area in between, but it tended to receive little attention.* For the most militant agencies, something like a four-stage sequence seems to have been followed. First, a period of organizing, with much publicity and great expectations everywhere. Second, the beginning of operations, with the onset of conflict between the agency and local government institutions with even greater publicity. Third, a period of counter attack from local government, not infrequently accompanied by conflict and difficulties, including accounting troubles, within the agency itself. Fourth, victory for the established institution, or at best, stalemate accompanied by bitterness and charges of betrayal.[21] (Emphasis added.)

The "large area in between," which received little attention, is apparently not included in the scope of Moynihan's study, and his unfavorable evaluation does not necessarily apply to most CAAs.

Another criticism of Moynihan's evaluation is that it does not accurately reflect the experience of the agencies examined. A detailed study of the experience of MFY came to a more balanced conclusion than Moynihan's assertion "Mobilization For Youth Lost." Alfred Fried's account of "The Attack on Mobilization" is summarized as follows:

> It is difficult to assess the actual effect the attack had on Mobilization's programs. The welfare-rights movement, the most successful and perhaps most controversial protest activity of the agency, occurred after the attack; the total budget of the agency for the

next program year increased; yet staff certainly were demoralized and the community-organization department practically ceased functioning for six months; relationships with the schools, never good, were further strained; and a few businesses cancelled their on-the-job training contract.[22]

Contrary to the impression left by Moynihan, MFY is still functioning, still benefits from city, state, and federal funds, and is still actively engaged in organizing the poor. In fact, it is now even more committed to a political strategy than ever before.[23]

Walter Grove and Herbert Costner have published an evaluation of the political strategy as it was implemented by the Central Area Motivation Program, an OEO agency in Seattle.[24] The object of the program was to organize neighborhood clubs that would serve as spokesmen for the poor residents in the community. The authors proceeded by interviewing the members listed in the clubs' records. Their findings were that many of the listed members were unaware of their membership, that neighborhood organization participants were most likely to be those who were active in the community before the club was formed, and that the organizations' goals were limited and remained unrealized. Their conclusion: "The strategy of organizing the poor described in this paper—an attempt to develop local neighborhood self-improvement associations through the efforts of an indigenous community organizer—was a failure."[25] However, they suggest that different tactics might improve the effectiveness of the political strategy. Their recommendations are that:

> An organizational focus around a common problem rather than a shared locality might provide a more realistic base for organizing the poor, and might also assist in recruiting a higher proportion of the hard core poor and a larger membership base. Involvement of professionals in relevant specialties and citizens other than the poor and near poor might assist in overcoming some of the other organizational problems by providing information and guidance as well as encouragement in the face of delayed achievement. [26]

Nonetheless, the basic finding of Grove and Costner is that the political strategy was a failure. With respect to the three criteria they found no evidence of change in the pattern of participation in decision-making by the poor in Seattle.

Francis Piven and Richard Cloward's study of the U.S. public welfare system provides a provocative evaluation of the Community Action Program. They argue that the War on Poverty (Great Society) programs, and particularly the CAP, significantly increased the financial resources available to the poor by enabling a larger number and proportion of them to receive public assistance:

91

When the families who showed up at a community-action agency asked for housing because they lived in rat infested tenements, or for more money for rent because they were dislocated by urban renewal, or for jobs, what were agency staff to do? They could not provide low-rent housing when none was being built or break down discriminatory housing patterns, or create jobs, or overcome discriminatory hiring practices. But it was possible to badger the welfare department into putting families on the relief rolls.

In other words, while the Great Society agencies often attempted to make gains for blacks in housing and health care and employment, resistance was stiff and sometimes virulent, for other groups in the cities had major stakes in these services and resources. But there were few other major groups in the cities with direct and immediate interests in welfare. Consequently, relief-giving turned out to be the most expeditious way to deal with the political pressures created by a dislocated poor, just as it had been many times in the past.[27]

Cloward and Piven also note that the War on Poverty programs led to the formation of the National Welfare Rights Organizations (NWRO), a group that institutionalized the influence of public assistance recipients and now functions as a lobby for the poor in Washington as well as in local communities.

In many respects the emergence of NWRO represents the most striking example one could give of the federal role in stimulating the welfare explosion. For what must be recognized is that the welfare poor came to form a coherent organization as a consequence of federal intervention in the cities.[28]

In terms of the three dimensions selected earlier to evaluate the political strategy, Cloward and Piven's analysis indicates that (1) the CAAs were not effective in expanding the scope of participation of the poor into established areas such as housing and employment, but that (2) they created a new issue, welfare rights, and (3) they significantly increased the political resources available to the poor by securing more money through public assistance and by stimulating the development of a permanent formal organization to articulate the interests of the welfare population.

Peter Bachrach and Morton Baratz have studied the CAP in Baltimore and its effect on that city's political process. They conclude that OEO programs significantly altered the position of the black population in the Baltimore power structure. Prior to the EOA, "the white majority in Baltimore thoroughly dominated the city's political system."[29] As a consequence,

As late as 1965 the political system in Baltimore was, for all practical purposes, closed to the people in the "dark ghetto," people who made up roughly 80% of the city's poverty population. In areas of vital concern to them—housing, employment and education—the poor had access neither to existing public agencies nor established arenas of conflict for redress of their grievances.[30]

According to Bachrach and Baratz the implementation of the CAP during the period 1966 to 1968 changed this situation. The authors find that by 1968, "So far as anti-poverty and race relations issues in Baltimore are concerned, there are no longer any insuperable barriers to entry into the decision-making arena."[31] The change is attributed to federal intervention in the form of antipoverty programs. The federal efforts provided the black poor with resources, a doctrine of legitimacy and financial incentives that helped them shift their power position. The authors conclude,

> To restate, federal programs and federal funds have been the main means, directly and indirectly, by which the black poor have gained a foothold in Baltimore's political system. The programs and money have helped directly by enforcing the administrative guidelines on citizen participation in planning and distributing services. They have helped indirectly in that the poor are increasingly being enlisted to support different local welfare agencies in their competition for a larger share of available funds.[32]

Ralph Kramer studied the CAPs in five California communities—Berkeley, Contra Costa County, Oakland, San Francisco, and Santa Clara County—with special attention to the decentralized neighborhood programs in the last three areas. Kramer found that "this experience of attempting to organize the poor in three communities demonstrated that it was possible, with the investment of a substantial number of staff, to organize and sustain for relatively short periods of time small neighborhood organizations that could involve a selected group of residents in a variety of self-help and neighborhood improvement activities."[33] In terms of the three criteria, the CAPs were able to organize groups to represent the poor. However, these groups had limited resources and did not develop new issues. In Kramer's words,

> The issues selected by these groups were generally of immediate local concern, represented the lowest common denominator of interest, and rarely involved the development of long-range plans. Usually engaged in seeking remedial action in a consensual manner

rather than through protest or direct action, most of these meliorative organizations were quite middle class in their character. . . . They demonstrated some ability to bring about minor adjustments and modifications in environmental conditions, but very few groups made the transition from a concern with social services to more political involvement.[34]

To summarize, the published studies of CAAs do not lead to any single conclusion. The findings are inconclusive. Bachrach and Baratz's study of Baltimore and, to a lesser degree, Cloward and Piven's study of the welfare system indicate that the CAP has had a recognizable effect on the political system in those places where CAAs pursued this objective. In contrast Costner and Grove's study of Seattle and Moynihan's study of New York and Syracuse found that CAAs pursuing the political strategy were virtually total failures. Finally, Kramer's study of California CAPs and Fried's study of New York's Mobilization for Youth yielded mixed results. No clear conclusion regarding the effectiveness of the political strategy can be drawn from the published studies.

The conflicting, and in some cases even contradictory, results of the published studies can be attributed to two sources—one methodological and one substantive. First, the case study approach, which is the method employed by each evaluator, is subject to each of the sources of invalidity described by Campbell and Stanley. This is particularly true for the four sources of invalidity discussed earlier in Chapter 4—history, maturation, differential selection, and experimental mortality.

Maturation and history—that is, the passage of time and/or unique events coterminous with the implementation of the CAP—might explain the reported success of Baltimore's CAA and/or the reported failure of Seattle's. The case studies used in each work allow no way to correct for the unique circumstances operating in each city and do not permit identification of the net contribution made by government intervention in the form of the CAP.

Certainly differential selection affected Moynihan's findings. He clearly selected for examination only those programs that were most militant in their approach (MFY and Syracuse) and did not randomly choose CAAs for his study. Thus the approaches used in the published studies are subject to significant methodological shortcomings that contribute to their conflicting findings.

Second, despite methodological faults, the finds of each of the studies in each of the cities may be correct. Government intervention may produce different results in different cities. The political strategy may be successful in Baltimore, but not in Seattle. This points to a need for comparative research to indicate why federal intervention produces different results in different cities.

In sum we have reviewed the published studies of the impact of the political strategy as implemented in the CAP and found that they do not give consistent support to any single conclusion. It is apparent that comparative research is necessary to overcome the methodological shortcomings inherent in the case study approach and to identify the factors that contribute to the differential impact of the CAP in various communities.

A COMPARATIVE ANALYSIS OF OEO DATA

In order to carry out the comparative analysis required to evaluate the impact of the CAP, two conditions must be met. First, we need a theory that suggests the factors that might explain the varying impacts of the CAPs in different cities. Second, we need a body of data that measures the independent variables set forth in the theory and dependent variables represented by our three criteria.

The important factors in determining differential impacts may be (1) the characteristics of the local community, particularly its political system, and (2) the nature of the intervention. Research by political scientists and sociologists points to the fact that cities differ significantly in their political structures.[35] Several related typologies have been developed to distinguish among forms of local government—commission, mayor-council (including "weak" mayor and "strong" mayor types), and city manager. Second, cities have been classified by their "political ethos"—private-regarding or public-regarding.[36] More relevant for our concern are typologies based on patterns of decision-making. Similar typologies have been developed by Terry Clark and Peter Rossi.[37] Clark divides cities into four theoretical types based upon two dimensions: the extent to which participation in decision-making is shared by many actors or limited to a few (elite versus mass participation) and the degree to which decision-making is fragmented into numerous issue areas or united into one homogeneous pattern. The four theoretical models produced by combining these dimensions are (1) monolithic, (2) polylithic, (3) pluralistic, and (4) mass participation. Roosi's similar classification scheme divides cities into (1) pyramidal, (2) polylith, (3) caucus rule, and (4) amorphus decision-making types.

The hypothesis that cities with different types of political structures and different types of decision-making patterns will produce different policy outputs has been the subject of considerable research. For example, Rosenthal and Crain have found the decision-making patterns are an important determinant of the success or failure of efforts to fluoridate a city's water supply.[38] They concluded,

> What we have found, we think, indicates that fluoridation has a better chance of consideration and adoption where the following conditions are met: there is a local political structure characterized by decision-making authority centralized in a relatively strong

executive like a manager or a partisan mayor; the political structure provides the mechanisms through forms of government and strong parties which insulate mayors and managers from "irregular" pressures likely to arise on this issue; and finally, that there is a low level of direct citizen participation both as a general rule and specifically on the fluoridation decision.[39]

Similarly, Lineberry and Fowler have found that "reformed" local governments (that is, those having nonpartisan elections, at-large constituencies, and manager governments) differ significantly from other cities in selected measures of policy outcomes.[40]

One systematic comparative study of the impact of community action programs has been published. Greenstone and Peterson studied the CAPs in Chicago, Philadelphia, New York, and Los Angeles.[41] They differentiated the political structures of the four cities on the basis of "dispersion of political power" as measured by the percentage of Democratic primary election contests (1958-64) in which losing candidates received at least 20 percent of the vote. They measured the impact of the CAP on the power of the poor in terms of the share of CAA governing board members who were chosen to represent the poor. The relationship between the two variables is presented in Chart 6.1. Their finding suggest that political structure of the city may be related to the CAP impact in a curvilinear fashion.

One hypothesis then is that the political strategy, particularly as manifest in the CAP, will have a different impact in different types of cities. It is possible to present this relationship in terms consistent with the existing comparative urban research and our criteria for judging the impact of the political strategy. One possibility is that the greater the degree of political pluralism existing in a city, the greater the change in the direction of pluralism a CAP will produce. Rephrased, this hypothesis states that the political strategy helps most where it is needed least. It reflects the belief that militant programs are likely to be quickly repressed in local communities where the poor do not already have some influence but can more easily expand the influence of the poor where they have already achieved some degree of political resources and participation. A second possibility is that the political strategy will produce the most change in cities where the poor have the least influence. This reflects the belief that CAPs can achieve significant breakthroughs in areas where the poor are most oppressed, but in cities where the poor already have some influence CAPs may be co-opted or otherwise prevented from increasing their political power. A third hypothesis is that the political strategy is most effective in cities falling in the middle range and least effective at the extremes.

The second set of factors that may explain the differential impact of the political strategy relates to the nature of the intervention. The CAP programs are not identical. An obvious factor that could explain their varying degrees of success is their size. Allocation of CAP funds has been

CHART 6.1

Political Structure of Cities and Impact
of CAP on Power of Poor

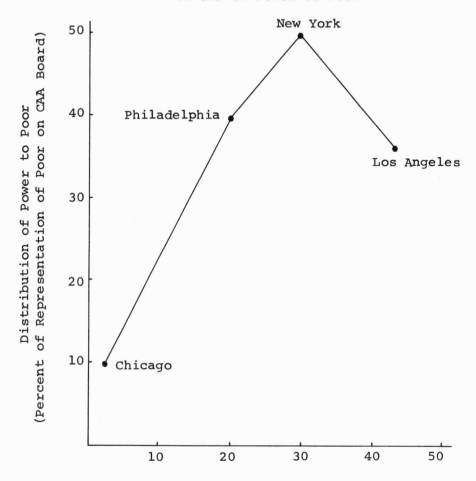

Dispersion of Power Existing in City
(Percent of Primary Contests in Which
Loser Received 20 Percent or More)

Source: Greenstone and Peterson, "Reformers,
Machines, and the War on Poverty," James Wilson, ed.,
City Politics and Public Policy (John Wiley and Sons:
New York, 1968), p. 283.

somewhat arbitrary. The level of funding varies considerably. New York receives the largest amount, well over $100 million annually, while other cities receive less than $1 million. More important is the fact that funding varies greatly even on a per capita basis. Levitan's analysis of grants to the 10 largest CAP agencies showed a range from $493 per poor person in New York to $276 in Pittsburgh.[42] Thus size of the program may be a critical factor in explaining program effectiveness.

Some research has been directed to the relationship between characteristics of areas and the size of their CAP in terms of dollars, but no study has related the size of the CAP to its impact in terms of redistributing political power. These studies demonstrate that variations in personal income, interparty competition, and political cultures are three environmental variables that have a positive relationship with CAP expenditures.[43]

A second dimension in which CAPs differ is the extent to which they have followed a political strategy. Evidence was presented to show that most CAAs engaged in some activities geared to the political strategy, but the proportion of resources so devoted varies substantially. One hypothesis is that a simple linear relationship exists; the greater the proportion of CAP resources devoted to political action the greater the change produced in the local power structure. The case studies suggest the following alternative hypothesis: Those CAAs devoting either a very high or a very low proportion of their resources to political activity are least likely to achieve change, while those in the middle range are most likely to be most effective. This hypothesis suggests that a mixture of service and political programs is the key to success.

In order for us to obtain data that might be useful in evaluating the political strategy, a review was made of reports submitted to the OEO as a result of contract research sponsored by that agency. One set of evaluations examined institutional change in four important areas: social service agencies, public schools, private business (employers), and neighborhood political organizations. Specific measures were developed for assessing change in each area. For education, 13 variables were used including (1) increase in number of minority members on school staff, (2) decrease in student-teacher ratio, (3) change in parent assessment of schools. For social service agencies 12 measures were used including (1) increase in the hiring of public training program graduates, (2) increase in the number of employees in the agency, (3) increase in total number of people served. For employers, eight variables were used including (1) increase in the hiring of public training program graduates, (2) increase in the number of employers advertising as "equal employment opportunity employer," (3) increase in the percent of unskilled workers who are black. In each of these three institutional sectors the variables used do not directly measure changes in decision-making practices. In this sense they do not gauge the success of the political strategy. However, they represent changes that are likely to occur if a city's poorer residents gain more influence in decision-making, indirectly they reflect the success of the political strategy.

In the fourth area, neighborhood political organizations, the five variables used do directly measure changes in decision-making patterns. The five variables are

(1) increase in level of organization and number of demands by residents;

(2) increase in participation of residents in electoral politics;

(3) voter registration drive and increase in registration;

(4) increase in percent of population who are members of community organizations; and

(5) increase in petitioning of public agencies by organizations.

These variables reflect increased participation through greater numbers of registered voters and increased electoral activity; greater resources for existing groups by expansion of the membership of community organizations; and the development of new issues through an increased number of demands by local organizations and an increase in the petitioning of public agencies by organizations.

Data to determine the impact of CAPs on these four sets of variables were gathered by the National Opinion Research Center (NORC) of the University of Chicago. NORC interviewers visited 50 cities with a population of 50,000 or more and spoke with CAA officials as well as representatives from each of the four institutional categories being examined. The NORC staff prepared four reports that were submitted to the OEO and are on file in the OEO national office but that have not been published.[44]

OEO evaluation officials also contracted with a private consulting firm, Barss, Reitzel, and Associates, Inc. (BR), of Cambridge, Massachusetts. BR was asked to perform an independent analysis of the data gathered by the NORC interviewers. Thus there are two independent interpretations of the survey data. Moreover, BR conducted its own research to explore in depth the effects of the CAP on political activity among the poor. Additional interviews were conducted by BR with between 5 and 10 leaders of organizations representing the poor in each of the 50 communities surveyed by NORC and further intensive interviewing was performed in 5 of the communities. BR sumbitted four reports to OEO as a result of its work. Like the NORC reports they are unpublished but are on file at the OEO national office.[45]

Finally, because the two groups arrived at similar conclusions they submitted a joint report in May 1970 to OEO, "The Impact of the Community Action Programs on Institutional Change: Assistance to Community Organizations as a Successful Strategy."

Both evaluations concluded that CAP was a modest success when judged on the basis of its ability to generate institutional change. Based on figures from the 50 cities and 4 institutional sectors, they concluded,

Reports from institutional leaders on CAPs role in increasing their responsiveness to the needs of the poor have followed similar patterns in each sector. Changes directly credited to CAP have tended to be auxiliary in nature (OJT, parent activity and more referrals) and not to involve basic transformations of institutional structures. These changes may be meaningful first steps toward a basic reordering of these institutions to provide more substantial satisfaction of the needs of the poor, but cannot be interpreted as a commitment to follow such an evolutionary course. Where "gut issues" (percent of blacks employed, non-graded instruction, and percent served who are on welfare) are concerned, CAP has had little impact.

For those who may have expected large institutions dealing with the poor to change in a relatively short time (five years) CAP must be judged a failure. For those who said that it would be impossible to effect any substantial change in these institutions, CAP should be judged as a viable agent of change. Several "surface" changes have been effected and some instances of substantial change have been reported.[46]

However, this represents a general finding based upon the average experience of all cities and sectors combined. We have already noted that there are substantial variations in the impact of CAPs among cities. NORC and BR data are significant because they permit further investigation of the hypotheses suggested earlier. They allow examination of the effect of the nature of the intervention and the preexisting condition of the political structure on the impact of the CAAs.

In examing the effect of the nature of the intervention on a CAAs effectiveness, both studies (BR and NORC) used similar methods. The cities were divided into three types based upon the general strategy pursued by the CAA:

(1) Education and social service goals: This is the traditional orientation, which we have called the service strategy.

(2) Organizational goals: This heavily emphasizes community organization and corresponds to the political strategy.

(3) Employment goals: This stresses training and job placement and for purposes of this study may be considered a variant of the service strategy.

The 50 cities were found to be distributed as follows: traditional, 17; organizational, 18; employment, 15.

The data from both studies support the hypothesis that the goal pursued by a city's CAA (that is, the nature of the intervention) is an important determinant of CAP effectiveness. For 9 of the 12 variables used to measure change in the social service sector, the CAAs with organizational goals scored the highest; in 8 of the 13 public school variables they were the highest; for one of the eight employer variables they were the highest (CAAs pursuing employment goals were highest in five); and in three of the five political organization variables they were the highest. The NORC study concluded,

> Cities in which the CAA emphasizes organizational goals are much more likely to be undergoing institutional changes than are cities in which the CAA emphasizes service goals. This is indicated by the fact that in twenty-one of the thirty-eight institutional change variables, the highest percent showing a high level of change is in the middle or "organizational" column. In only three instances is the highest percent in the traditional column. In another twelve instances the employment column shows the highest percent of change. There are two ties for the highest percent change.[47]

Similarly the BR study concluded,

> The one CAA characteristic almost universally associated with CAP impact is a heavy emphasis on community organization as a goal. This finding is provocative. It substantiates the *a priori* hypothesis that community political activity might be a more productive strategy for inducing institutional change than activities oriented towards the needs of individuals.[48]

The significance of the CAA goal stands out if we examine the change in political institutions, the sector most accurately reflecting the impact of the political strategy. Data from the NORC survey are presented in Table 6.4. Two of the variables in which organizational CAAs scored highest (1 and 5) reflect increased demands and petitioning by poor citizens. This indicates that the political strategy is effective in bringing new issues into public consideration and supports Bachrach and Baratz's similar findings in Baltimore. The third variable in which organizational CAAs score highest relates to membership in community organizations. This indicates the CAP is helpful in adding resources (in the form of membership) to local organizations and thereby enabling them to participate more effectively in community decision-making.

The two variables on which organizational CAAs did not score highest relate to voter registration and electoral politics. The CAAs do not seem to be effective in enhancing the influence of the poor in traditional electoral politics, but they do improve their position in other areas of local decision-making.

The evidence from these studies supports the hypothesis that the nature of the intervention is an important determinant of CAA effectiveness. Those agencies giving greater emphasis to the political strategy had greater success in securing political and institutional change.

The data gathered by BR in its supplementary interviews with local political groups provide additional insights into the impact of CAAs on local

TABLE 6.4

**Percent of CAAs Scoring High on Political
Change Variables**

	Traditional CAAs	Employment CAAs	Organizational CAAs
1. Increase in level of organization and number of demands by residents	0	0	35
2. Increase in partici- pation of residents in electoral politics	25	38	12
3. Voter registration drive and increase in voter registration	47	60	50
4. Increase in percent of population who are members of community organizations	25	8	33
5. Increase in petition- ing of public agencies by organizations	25	54	56

Source: National Opinion Research Center, "Community Organization Efforts, Political and Institutional Change, and the Diffusion of Change Produced by Community Action Programs" (Chicago, April 1970), Table 2.1, pp. 31-32.

political structures. BR found that CAAs served the important function of developing leadership for indigenous groups. It concluded,

> One of the early problems encountered in CAP was the paucity of indigenous ghetto and poor white leadership with which to work. Current information indicates that this vacumm has been at least partially filled by leaders with a high degree of contact with CAP—if not indeed created by it. Most importantly, the leaders

who are associated with CAP tend to be more hopeful of institutional changes, less alienated from local governments, and attitudinally better prepared to act as instigators of change. Indeed, our data generally suggest that where CAP contacts with the poor population are frequent, residents tend to be less alienated and more hopeful that normal political processes can accomplish the changes needed to improve their daily existence. . . . Contact with CAP apparently has encouraged development of leaders who are oriented towards a non-violent, cooperative approach to the total community. Hopefully, over the long term, they will prove to be a vibrant, viable political source for change.[49]

Since we noted earlier that leadership is a particularly important resource for groups seeking to participate in local decision-making, this finding indicates the significance of CAAs in expanding the resources available to indigenous groups.

The supplementary interviews conducted by BR also provide data with which to assess the relationship between the existing political structure in a community and the impact of a CAA. The BR investigators examined several key variables: (1) the nature of the existing political organizations serving the poor; (2) the nature of public opinion among constituents of the existing political organizations; (3) the general nature of the CAA in the city; (4) the number of militant acts (demonstrations) undertaken by the CAA; and (5) the level of institutional change.

Table 6.5 summarizes the patterns of relationships found among these variables for each type of CAA (traditional, organizational, and employment). The BR findings support the hypothesis, suggested earlier, that CAAs produce the greatest change in areas where participation of the poor is already most developed. The most political CAAs were found in cities with larger and more active political organizations to represent the poor and where public opinion was already mobilized. These political agencies were the ones most effective in securing institutional changes. In contrast, traditional social service CAAs are found in cities with inactive, nonminority organizations representing the poor and with an unaroused public opinion. They engaged in no militant acts and achieved few institutional changes. The employment-oriented CAAs seem to represent a middle ground.

SUMMARY

This chapter examined the nature of the CAP and its effectiveness in executing the political strategy. It was found that the "maximum feasible participation" clause of Title II of the EOA was given three meanings, each of which was implemented in varying degrees among the more than 1,000

TABLE 6.5

Patterns of Community Political Activity

Type of CAA	Nature of Political Organizations	Nature of Public Opinion	CAA Activity	Level of Militant Acts	Institutional Changes
Traditional	Old, large, white, inactive	Unaroused	Small, little activity	None	Few
Employment	Young, black, active, low alliance	Politicized	High employment service	High in area of employment	Medium in employment and social services
Organizational	Young, black, active, many alliances	Politicized, mobilized	Organization emphasis	Higher in all areas	High in all areas

Source: Barrs, Reitzel, and Associates, "Community Action and Institutional Change," Report to the Office of Economic Opportunity (Cambridge, Mass., July 1969), Table I-1, p. I-15.

CAAs. A political strategy emphasizing organization of the poor was only one of the interpretations of the requirements of the act, and this strategy was given great emphasis in relatively few CAAs. However, most agencies did devote some of their resources to pursuing the political strategy.

An analysis of published studies of CAAs in several cities found conflicting conclusions. Some investigators found the program had either no impact or an unfavorable impact on the influence of the poor in local decision-making. Others found that the CAP was of vital importance in helping the poor press new issues and gain added influence in community decision-making.

The conflicting results were attributed to the methodological weakness of the case study approach, which does not permit the researcher to control for extraneous factors influencing outcomes. It was hypothesized that two sets of factors—the existing political structure in the city and the nature of the CAA intervention—were not controlled in the case studies and contribute to the diverse findings.

Comparative data obtained from unpublished contract research, including a survey of 50 CAAs, were analyzed to provide evidence to explore the hypothesized relationships. The data supported the hypothesis that the nature of the intervention was important. CAAs that attached greater emphasis to the political strategy were more successful in securing political change. The contract studies also indicated that the existing political structure was an important factor. The stronger the existing organizations representing the poor, the more likely the CAA would emphasize organizational goals and achieve institutional change.

NOTES

1. *Community Action Program Guide,* Community Action Program, Office of Economic Opportunity, (Washington, D.C., 1965), p. 16.

2. See Frank Riessman and Arthur Pearl, *New Careers for the Poor* (New York: The Free Press, 1965); and Frank Riessman and Hermine Popper, *Up from Poverty: New Career Ladders for Nonprofessionals* (New York: Harper & Row, 1968).

3. Daniel Yankelovich, Inc., "A Study of the Nonprofessional in the Community Action Program" (New York, September 1966).

4. *Ibid.,* p. 15.

5. *CAP Guide,* Section B.6.

6. John Wofford, "The Politics of Local Responsibility: Administration of the Community Action Program, 1964-1966," in James L. Sundquist, ed., *On Fighting Poverty* (New York: Basic Books, 1969), p. 82.

7. Daniel Yankelovich, Inc., "A Study of the Effects of Sections 210 and 211 of the 1967 Amendments to the EOA as Required Under Section 233(c) of the Amendments" (New York, February 1969), three volumes.

8. Paul Petersen, "Forms of Representation: Participation of the Poor in the Community Action Program," *American Political Science Review* (June 1970), pp. 491-507.

9. *Ibid.*, p. 492.

10. *Ibid.*, p. 505.

11. Kenneth Clark and Jeannette Hopkins, *A Relevant War Against Poverty* (New York: Harper & Row, 1969).

12. *Ibid.*, pp. 60-61.

13. H. W. Hallman, "The Community Action Program: An Interpretative Analysis," in W. Bloomberg and H. Schmandt, eds., *Power, Poverty and Urban Policy,* Urban Affairs Annual Review No. 2, (Beverly Hills, Cal.: Sage Publications, 1968), pp. 287-89. See also U.S. Senate, Committee on Labor and Public Welfare, Subcommittee on Employment, Manpower, and Poverty, *Examination of the War on Poverty: Community Action Program,* Vol. IV (Washington, D.C., 1967), pp. 97-915.

14. Stephen M. Rose, *The Betrayal of the Poor: The Transformation of Community Action* (Cambridge, Mass.: Schenkman, 1972).

15. James Sundquist, *Making Federalism Work* (Washington, D.C.: The Brookings Institution, 1969).

16. *Ibid.*, pp. 61-62. The OEO study referred to is apparently that by Clark and Hopkins.

17. Peter Eisinger, "The Anti-Poverty Community Action Group as a Political Force in the Ghetto" (unpublished Ph.D. dissertation, Political Science Department, Yale University, 1969), p. 113.

18. Martin Luther King, Jr., Neighborhood Health Center, *Third Annual Report,* December 31, 1969, p. 102.

19. See Richard M. Pious, "Policy and Public Administration: The Legal Services Program in the War on Poverty," *Politics and Society* 1, 3 (May 1971), 365-92.

20. Daniel P. Moynihan, *Maximum Feasible Misunderstanding: Community Action in the War on Poverty* (New York: The Free Press, 1969), pp. 134-35.

21. *Ibid.*, p. 131.

22. Alfred Fried, "The Attack on Mobilization," in Harold Weissman, ed., *Community Development in the Mobilization for Youth Experience* (New York: Association Press, 1969), pp. 161-62.

23. On this point see Harold Weissman, "Overview of the Community Development Program," in Weissman, ed., *Community Development*, p. 28, where Weissman describes the fourth and latest stage of MFY's development as follows: "Phase four represented the beginning of the idea that community development, or the strategy of involving local people in planning for and influencing their own communities, should not be a separate program in an agency like Mobilization. Rather, the agency itself should be viewed as a community development agency, with all of its programs, activities, and services geared to community development."

24. Walter Grove and Herbert Costner, "Organizing the Poor: An Evaluation of a Strategy," *Social Science Quarterly*, December 1969, pp. 643-56.

25. *Ibid.*, p. 654.

26. *Ibid.*, p. 655.

27. Frances F. Piven and Richard A. Cloward, *Regulating the Poor: The Functions of Public Welfare* (New York: Pantheon, 1971), p. 289.

28. *Ibid.*, p. 329.

29. Peter Bachrach and Morton Baratz, *Power and Poverty: Theory and Practice* (New York: Oxford University Press, 1970), p. 69.

30. *Ibid.*, p. 69.

31. *Ibid.*, p. 96.

32. *Ibid.*, p. 99.

33. Ralph Kramer, *Participation of the Poor* (Englewood Cliffs, N.J.: Prentice-Hall, 1969), p. 237.

34. *Ibid.*, pp. 237-38.

35. A useful summary of this research is Bret Hawkins, *Politics and Urban Policies* (Indianapolis: Bobbs-Merrill, 1971).

36. See Edward Banfield and James Wilson, *City Politics* (New York: Vintage, 1963).

37. Terry Clark, "Social Stratification, Differentiation and Integration," in Terry Clark, ed., *Community Structure and Decision-Making* (San Francisco: Chandler, 1968), pp. 25-44; and Peter H. Rossi, "Power and Community Structures," in Clark, ed., *Community Structure and Decision-Making*, pp. 129-38.

38. Robert Crain, Elihu Katz, and Donald Rosenthal, *The Politics of Community Conflict* (Indianapolis: Bobbs-Merrill, 1969).

39. Robert Crain and Donald Rosenthal, "Structures and Values in Local Political Systems," *Journal of Politics*, February 1966, pp. 169-96. Also reprinted in Clark, ed., *Community Structure and Decision-Making*, pp. 215-42; and James Wilson, ed., *City Politics and Public Policy* (New York: John Wiley & Sons, 1968), pp. 217-42.

40. Robert Lineberry and Edmund Fowler, "Reformism and Public Policies in American Cities," in Wilson, ed., *City Politics and Public Policy,* pp. 97-123.

41. J. David Greenstone and Paul E. Peterson, "Reformers, Machines and the War on Poverty" in James Wilson, ed., *City Politics and Public Policy,* (John Wiley & Sons, New York, 1968), pp. 267-92.

42. Sar Levitan, *The Great Society's Poor Law: A New Approach to Poverty* (Baltimore: The Johns Hopkins Press, 1969), p. 120.

43. Joseph Cepuran, "CAP Expenditures in the Fifty States: A Comparison," *Urban Affairs Quarterly,* March 1969, pp. 325-41.

44. The titles and dates of these unpublished reports to OEO prepared by the National Opinion Research Center (NORC, Chicago) are "National Evaluation of Urban Community Action Programs," June 1969; "Community Mobilization and Institutional Change: The Influence of the CAP in Large Cities," August 1969; "Community Action Programs as Agents of Change in the Private Welfare Sector," August 1969; and "Community Organization Efforts, Political and Institutional Change, and the Diffusion of Change Produced by Community Action Programs," April 1970.

45. The titles and dates of these unpublished reports to the OEO prepared by Barss, Rietzel, and Associates (Cambridge, Mass.) are "Attributes of Successful Community Action Programs," March 1968; "Community Action and Institutional Change," July 1969; "Mobilizing Poor Communities," 1970; "Community Action and Urban Institutional Change," August 1970.

46. Barss, Rietzel and Associates, "Community Action and Institutional Change," pp. I-16-I-17.

47. NORC, "Community Organization Efforts," p. 28.

48. Barss, Rietzel, and Associates, "Community Action and Institutional Change," p. I-8.

49. *Ibid.,* pp. I-19-I-20.

7

CONCLUSIONS

SUMMARY OF FINDINGS

This analysis has examined the impact of federal antipoverty policies. It began by placing the study of the impact of governmental actions in the context of the systems model of political life elaborated by David Easton. This model permits the study of policy outputs as either a dependent or an independent variable. Some work has been done in studying the factors influencing antipoverty policy outputs, but very little research has been devoted to the study of these policies as an independent variable. This study examines the effects of federal antipoverty programs.

Two general policies or strategies were identified as the principal means employed by the federal government to deal with domestic poverty. One, the service strategy, assumes that the poor differ in some way from the majority who are not so afflicted and that these differences stem from individual deficiencies that can be overcome through the provision of remedial services. Since employment is the most commonly accepted means of self-support, the inability of the poor to secure employment is often pointed to as their major deficiency. Consequently, vocational training is a primary component of the service strategy. The second general policy, the political strategy, assumes that certain segments of the population are poor because they lack political power. Political power is equated with the functioning of well-organized groups, and the strategy looks to the formation and support of indigenous organizations to represent the interests of the poor as the preferred solution.

Specific pieces of legislation can be identified with each of these strategies. The Manpower Development and Training Act (MDTA) of 1962 represents the service strategy. Through legislative amendment and administrative changes this bill has become a part of the federal War on Poverty. It seeks to reduce poverty by training individuals below the poverty line for specific occupations and then placing them in jobs that will permit them to raise their previously low incomes. No piece of legislation can be completely identified with the political strategy, but it was found that Title II (the Community Action Program, CAP) of the Economic Opportunity Act (EOA) of 1963 did encourage and financially support political organization as well as other types of activities as a means of reducing poverty.

The criteria developed for evaluating the impact of the MDTA as an antipoverty program are (1) the program's "vertical target efficiency"—that is, the degree to which the program is used by the poor rather than other (nonpoor) groups; (2) the extent to which the poor have been able to utilize successfully the training services—that is, their completion or "graduation" rate; and (3) the income gains attributable to the successful participation in training programs. The criteria suggested for evaluating the CAP were derived from studies of decision-making in local communities and consist of (1) the degree of expanded participation of the poor in issue areas from which they formerly were excluded; (2) the level of additional resources provided to poverty groups to enhance their participation in issue areas already on the public's agenda; and (3) the development of new issues that were previously considered as nondecisions in a local community.

Analysis of the impact of the MDTA training program found that data were not available to evaluate properly its antipoverty effects. Data gathered by program administrators do not include the poverty status of enrollees, follow-up data by wage levels, or comparisons with appropriate control groups. Evaluation of the program's vertical efficiency must be based on data indirectly related to poverty status such as race, nature of household, and age. Using these indirect indicators one could estimate that poor individuals represent about half of all trainees in institutional training programs and an even smaller fraction of those in on-the-job training (OJT) programs. With respect to completion rates, data from a national sample of enrollees and a smaller sample of trainees in Michigan indicate that poor and nonpoor individuals have equal completion rates of about two-thirds. Data from two large-scale follow-up surveys indicate that training programs have raised the incomes of graduates, particularly the incomes of previously poor trainees. However, both these surveys included only those completers who secured employment and excluded those remaining unemployed, and neither compared the income gains of graduates to those of a control group. One additional national survey, which utilized a control group and incorporated the experiences of all completers, found no significant change in wage rates but did find a slight gain in the amount of employment (hours per week) secured by completers. Thus the evidence is inconclusive but does indicate some slight gain for those completing training.

Analysis of the impact of the CAP also found significant data gaps. The Office of Economic Opportunity (OEO) does not gather information about the political impact of local community action agencies (CAAs). Data had to be drawn from a special National Opinion Research Center (NORC) survey and case studies of selected communities. Published case studies of several communities, including New York, Baltimore, Seattle, San Francisco, and Syracuse, yielded inconclusive findings. In some areas—for example, Baltimore—researchers attributed significant transformations in decision-making patterns to the implementation of the CAP. In other cases, such as Seattle and Syracuse, researchers found no significant changes in decision-making patterns as a result of the CAP. Finally, in New York, scholars reached differing conclusions regarding the impact of the CAP.

The differing and inconclusive findings can in part be attributed to the methodological shortcomings of the case study approach. This technique does not allow control for sources of invalidity arising from the influence of excluded factors. Consequently, a comparative study was undertaken to include two critical variables—the nature of the CAP intervention and the preexisting political relationships. Data from a NORC survey of 50 CAP cities indicated that in cities where political organization was stressed by the local CAA, there was more likely to be a change in the resources (particularly membership) of indigenous groups, and new issues were more likely to emerge as a result of petitioning and presentation of demands by groups representing the poor. Interview data also indicated that communities that had a more pluralistic pattern of decision-making prior to the emergence of the CAP were more likely to have experienced changes in the existing patterns as a result of the CAP.

IMPLICATIONS OF FINDINGS

At the beginning of this study it was anticipated that a proper evaluative framework together with relevant data would permit one to reach definitive conclusions regarding the relative effectiveness of the political strategy and the service strategy, at least as they were represented in the EOA and the MDTA. However, we found that required data were not available either from the agencies involved in administering these programs or from contract or independent studies. Hence, the first and perhaps the most important conclusion from our research is that government agencies have neglected the problems of program (and policy) analysis and evaluation. Consequently, little is known and little can be learned at this time about the impact of these new government efforts.

This finding supports the conclusion of a 1970 study by the staff of the Urban Institute on *Federal Evaluation Policy*. This study reviewed program evaluation activities in four federal agencies: the Department of Housing and Urban Development, the Office of Economic Opportunity, the Department of Health, Education, and Welfare, and the Department of Labor. Their judgment on the caliber of and commitment to evaluation efforts is summarized as follows:

> The most impressive finding about the evaluation of social programs in the federal government is that substantial work in this field has been almost nonexistent.
>
> Few significant studies have been undertaken. Most of those carried out have been poorly conceived. Many small studies around the country have been carried out with such lack of uniformity of design and objective that the results rarely are comparable or responsive to the questions facing policy makers. . . .
>
> The impact of activities that cost the public millions, sometimes billions, of dollars has not been measured. One cannot point with confidence to the difference, if any, that most social programs cause in the lives of Americans.[1]

Clearly, there is need for greater efforts to analyze the impact of government programs—both within and outside of government. One priority area is the development of better performance measures. The recent emphasis on a planning programing budgeting system (PPBS) in federal and state government as well as the increasing interest of scholars in performance budgeting is resulting in some progress, but much remains to be done.[2] The present situation has been accurately described by an advisory group within the Department of HEW:

> Many of our statistics on social problems are merely a by-product of the informational requirements of routine management. This by-product process does not usually produce the information that we most need for policy or scholarly purposes, and it means that our supply of statistics has an accidental and imbalanced character.[3]

Some guidelines for developing new and better performance measures have been suggested by Alice Rivlin.[4] First, since programs are likely to have more than one output, multiple output measures are necessary. The use of multiple performance measures will help prevent distorted assessments resulting from people trying to "beat the system," as in the coaching of pupils who are to take standardized tests. Second, Rivlin suggests measures must be related to the problem to be solved. "If absolute levels of performance are rewarded, then schools will select the brightest students, training programs will admit only the workers who will be easiest to place in jobs, health centers will turn away or neglect the hopelessly ill. To avoid these distortions, social service effectiveness must always be measured in relation to the difficulty of the task."[5]

A second effort needed to improve the study of the impact of government efforts is the formulation of systematic experimental designs. The case for this approach has been argued by Cain and Hollister:

> Social action programs are undertaken because there is a clearly perceived social problem that requires some form of amelioration. In general (with the exception perhaps of the area of medical drugs where a counter tradition has been carefully or painfully built up), we are not willing to postpone large-scale attempts at amelioration of such problems until all the steps of a careful testing of hypotheses, development of pilot projects, etc., have been carried out.... We would suggest that large-scale ameliorative social action and intentional experimentation are not incompatible; that experimental designs can be built into a large-scale social action program.
>
> If we begin a large national program with a frank awareness that we do not know which program concept is more likely to be most efficacious, then several program models could be selected for implementation in several areas, with enough variability in the key elements which make up the concepts to allow good measures of the differential response to those elements. If social action programs are approached with an "intentionally experimental" point of view, then the analytic powers of our statistical models of evaluation can be greatly enhanced by attempts to insure that "confounding" effects are minimized—i.e., that program treatment variables are uncorrelated with participant characteristics and particular types of environments.[6]

Perhaps the best-known example of this approach is the New Jersey Graduated Work Incentive Experiment funded by the OEO. It is an effort to determine how a negative income tax will affect work incentives among the poor and near poor. The project encompasses eight different combinations of income guarantees and work incentives among carefully selected groups and includes observation of a control group whose members receive no payment (except a small sum for reporting and providing information).

Third, researchers should follow the suggestion of Weiss and Rein to develop new evaluation methods. The less quantitative and more process-oriented techniques they advocate are not yet clearly defined, but alternatives to the experimental model should be considered for broad-aim programs that cannot be implemented through stable organizations in a controlled environments.

It is appropriate in this concluding section to return to the Eastonian model of the political system with which we began the study. In this context, one of our important findings is that in the American system little effort is made to determine the impact of governmental policy. This suggests that the feedback link within the political system may be weaker than theorists have assumed. This point requires elaboration.

In his *A Framework for Political Analysis,* Easton described three types of feedback information essential if a system is to cope successfully with environmental stress. He described the three types of feedback as follows:

> It is clear that, first, the authorities in the system, those invested with special responsibilities and powers to act in the name of the system, would need to know the conditions prevailing in the environment. . . .
>
> Second, the authorities must also seek to acquire information about the supportive state of mind of the members and the demands being voiced at least by the politically influential members of the system. . . .
>
> Third, the authorities must obtain information about the effects which the outputs have already produced. But for this, the authorities would have to act in perpetual darkness. There must be a continuous flow of information back to them so that whatever their goals may be with respect to support or the fulfillment of demands, they are aware of the extent to which their prior or current outputs have succeeded in achieving these goals.[8]

The third type of feedback information corresponds closely to the type of information represented by policy analysis. Policy analysis seeks to "obtain information about the effects which the outputs have already produced." The findings of this study indicate that this component of the feedback loop is a weak, though not missing, link in the American political system.

What are the consequences for a political system of inadequate feedback mechanisms of the type described? Easton has this to offer:

> Regardless of the specific goals of the authorities there must be a flow of information of the kinds described coming back to them. Only on the basis of knowledge of what has taken place or about the current state of affairs with respect to demand and supports would authorities be able to respond by adjusting, modifying, or correcting previous decisions, including the failure to make a decision. Not that they must do so; but at least possession of the

information provides them with the opportunity if they desire to use it. *Without such feedback, behavior would be erratic or random, unrelated in any causal way to what had previously occurred.*[9] (Emphasis added.)

Evidence of such "erratic and random" behavior, perhaps resulting from inadequate feedback information, can be drawn from the contemporary American political scene. New domestic programs are initiated and then expanded or cut back with little knowledge of their true impact. Congress is often in the position of having to determine appropriations with only common sense estimates of how additional funds will help alleviate specific problems. This point is underscored by the following testimony of an HEW official:

I remember being astonished when we started that study [of child health programs] that doctors could produce no evidence that children who saw doctors regularly were healthier than children who did not. They all believed it (and I do too) but they did not have any statistics to prove it. I was equally astonished to find that educators have little or no evidence that children who get more expensive education (newer buildings, higher paid teachers, etc.) learn more than children who get less expensive education. They believe (and so do I), but the available statistics do not prove it, nor does presently available information give any solid clues about what kinds of schools are best, or whether particular educational methods are more effective than others.[10]

If the American political system is to persist by coping with perceived environmental stress through positive action, it will require improved feedback mechanisms. This can be achieved in part by expanded and improved policy analysis in and out of government.

NOTES

1. Joseph S. Wholey, *et al., Federal Evaluation Policy* (Washington, D.C.: The Urban Institute, 1970), p. 15.

2. See Allen Schick, "The Road to PPB: The Stages of Budget Reform," *Public Administration Review* 26, December 1966, pp. 243-58; also his *Budget Innovation in the States* (Washington, D.C.: The Brookings Institution, 1971).

3. *Toward a Social Report*, U.S. Department of Health, Education, and Welfare (Washington, D.C., 1969), p. 96.

115

4. Alice Rivlin, *Systematic Thinking for Social Action* (Washington, D.C.: The Brookings Institution, 1971); also see her *Making Federal Programs Work Better*, Brookings Research Report 112 (Washington, D.C.: The Brookings Institution, 1971).

5. Rivlin, *Making Federal Programs Work Better*, p. 9.

6. Glen C. Cain and Robinson G. Hollister, "The Methodology of Evaluating Social Action Programs," in Peter Rossi and Walter Williams, eds., *Evaluating Social Programs* (New York: Seminar Press, 1972).

7. Robert Weiss and Martin Rein, "The Evaluation of Broad-Aim Programs," *Annals*, September 1969, pp. 133-42. See also *Ibid.*, pp. 86-87.

8. David Easton, *A Framework for Political Analysis* (Englewood Cliffs, N.J.: Prentice-Hall, 1965), pp. 128-29.

9. *Ibid.*, p. 129.

10. Alice Rivlin, "The Planning, Programming Budgeting System in the Department of Health, Education and Welfare: Some Lessons from Experience," in U.S. Congress, Joint Economic Committee, *The Analysis and Evaluation of Public Expenditures: The PPB System,* Vol. 3 (Washington, D.C. 1969), p. 917.

BIBLIOGRAPHY

BOOKS

Alinsky, Saul. *Reveille for Radicals*. New York: Vintage 1969.

Bachrach, Peter. *The Theory of Democratic Elitism*. Boston: Little, Brown, 1967.

——, and Morton Baratz. *Power and Poverty: Theory and Practice*. New York: Oxford University Press, 1970.

Banfield, Edward. *Political Influence*. Glencoe, Ill.: The Free Press, 1961.

——, and James Wilson. *City Politics*. New York: Vintage, 1963.

Bibby, John, and Roger Davidson. *On Capitol Hill: Studies in the Legislative Process*. New York: Holt, Rinehart and Winston, 1967.

Bloomberg, Warner, and Henry Schmandt, eds. *Power, Poverty and Urban Policy*. Beverly Hills, Cal.: Sage Publications, 1968.

Bolino, August. *Manpower and the City*. Cambridge, Mass.: Schenkman, 1969.

Burlage, Robb. *New York City's Municipal Hospitals: A Policy Review*. Washington, D.C.: Institute for Policy Studies, 1967.

Campbell, Donald, and Julian Stanley. *Experimental and Quasi-Experimental Designs for Research*. Chicago: Rand McNally, 1963.

Carmichael, Stokely, and Charles Hamilton. *Black Power*. New York: Vintage, 1967.

Clark, Kenneth. *Dark Ghetto*. New York: Harper & Row, 1965.

——, and Jeanette Hopkins. *A Relevant War Against Poverty*. New York: Harper & Row, 1969.

Clark, Terry, ed. *Community Structure and Decision Making*. San Francisco: Chandler Publishers, 1968.

Committee for Economic Development. *Raising Low Incomes Through Improved Education*. New York: The Committee, 1968.

——. *Training and Jobs for the Urban Poor*. New York: The Committee, 1970.

Crain, Robert, Elihu Katz, and Donald Rosenthal. *The Politics of Community Conflict.* Indianapolis: Bobbs-Merrill, 1969.

Dahl, Robert. *Modern Political Analysis.* Englewood Cliffs, N.J.: Prentice-Hall, 1963.

———. *Pluralist Democracy in the United States.* Chicago: Rand McNally, 1967.

———. *Who Governs?* New Haven, Conn.: Yale University Press, 1961.

Davies, Morton, and Vaughn Lewis. *Models of Political Systems.* New York: Praeger Publishers, 1971.

Dolbeare, Kenneth, and James Davis. *Little Groups of Neighbors.* Chicago: Markam, 1970.

Donovan, John. *The Politics of Poverty.* New York: Pegasus, 1967.

Downs, Anthony. *Who Are the Urban Poor?* New York: Committee for Economic Development, 1970.

Dye, Thomas. *Politics, Economics, and the Public.* Chicago: Rand McNally, 1966.

Easton, David. *A Framework for Political Analysis.* Englewood Cliffs, N.J.: Prentice-Hall, 1965.

———. *A Systems Analysis of Political Life.* New York: John Wiley & Sons, 1965.

———, ed. *Varieties of Political Theory.* Englewood Cliffs, N.J.: Prentice-Hall, 1966.

Ellis, William. *White Ethics and Black Power.* Chicago: Aldine, 1969.

Gans, Herbert. *The Urban Villagers.* New York: The Free Press, 1962.

Gittell, Marilyn. *Participants and Participation.* New York: Center for Urban Education, 1966.

Green, Phillip, and Sanford Levenson, eds. *Power and Community.* New York: Vintage, 1970.

Greer, Scott. *Urban Renewal and American Cities.* New York: Bobbs-Merrill, 1965.

Harrington, Michael. *The Other America.* Baltimore: Penguin Books, 1963.

Hawkins, Bret. *Politics and Urban Policies.* Indianapolis: Bobbs-Merrill, 1971.

Kaplan, Harold. *Urban Renewal Politics: Slum Clearance in Newark.* New York: Columbia University Press, 1963.

Kaufman, Herbert, and Wallace Sayre. *Governing New York City: Politics in the Metropolis.* New York: W. W. Norton, 1965.

Kershaw, Joseph. *Government Against Poverty.* Washington, D.C.: The Brookings Institution, 1970.

Kramer, Ralph. *Participation of the Poor.* Englewood Cliffs, N.J.: Prentice-Hall, 1969.

Lasswell, Harold. *Politics: Who Gets What, When and How.* New York: McGraw-Hill, 1936.

——, and Abraham Kaplan. *Power and Society: A Framework for Political Inquiry* New Haven, Conn.: Yale University Press, 1950.

——, and David Lerner, eds. *The Policy Sciences.* Stanford, Cal.: Stanford University Press, 1960.

Levine, Robert. *The Poor Ye Need Not Have With You.* Cambridge: Massachusetts Institute of Technology Press, 1970.

Levitan, Sar. *The Design of Federal Anti-Poverty Strategy.* Ann Arbor; Mich.: Institute of Labor and Industrial Relations, 1967.

——. *The Great Society's Poor Law: A New Approach to Poverty.* Baltimore: The Johns Hopkins Press, 1969.

——. *Federal Aid to Depressed Areas.* Baltimore: The Johns Hopkins Press, 1964.

——, and Garth Mangum. *Federal Training and Work Programs in the Sixties.* Ann Arbor, Mich.: Institute of Labor and Industrial Relations, 1969.

——, Garth Mangum, and Robert Taggart. *Economic Opportunity in the Ghetto: The Partnership of Government and Business.* Baltimore: The Johns Hopkins Press, 1970.

Lowi, Theodore. *At the Pleasure of the Mayor.* New York: The Free Press, 1964.

McCoy, Charles, and John Playford, eds. *Apolitical Politics.* New York: Thomas Crowell, 1967.

Mangum, Garth. *The Emergence of Manpower Policy.* New York: Holt, Rinehart and Winston, 1969.

Marris, Peter, and Martin Rein. *Dilemmas of Social Reform: Poverty and Community Action in the United States.* New York: Atherton Press 1967.

Martin, Roscoe, et al. *Decisions in Syracuse.* Bloomington: Indiana University Press, 1961.

Moynihan, Daniel. *Maximum Feasible Misunderstanding: Community Action in the War on Poverty.* New York: The Free Press, 1969.

——, ed. *On Understanding Poverty: Prospectives from the Social Sciences,* New York: Basic Books, 1969.

Piven, Frances, and Richard Cloward. *Regulating the Poor.* New York: Pantheon, 1971.

Polsby, Nelson. *Community Power and Political Theory.* New Haven, Conn.: Yale University Press, 1963.

Ranney, Austin, ed. *Political Science and Public Policy*. Chicago: Markham, 1968.

Ribich, Thomas. *Education and Poverty*. Washington, D.C.: The Brookings Institution, 1968.

Riessman, Frank, and Arthur Pearl. *New Careers for the Poor*. New York: The Free Press, 1965.

Riessman, Frank, and Hermine Popper. *Up from Poverty: New Career Ladders for Non-Professionals*. New York: Harper & Row, 1968.

Rivlin, Alice. *Making Federal Programs Work Better*. Washington, D.C.: The Brookings Institution, 1971.

——. *Systematic Thinking for Social Action*. Washington, D.C.: The Brookings Institution, 1971.

Rogers, David. *110 Livingston Street*. New York: Random House, 1968.

Rose, Arnold. *The Power Structure*. New York: Oxford University Press, 1967.

Rose, Stephen. *The Betrayal of the Poor*. Cambridge, Mass.: Shenkman, 1972.

Rossi, Peter, and Robert Dentler. *The Politics of Urban Renewal*. New York: The Free Press, 1961.

Rossi, Peter, and William Walter, eds. *Evaluating Social Programs*. New York: Seminar Press, 1972.

Samuelson, Paul. *Economics: An Introductory Analysis*. New York: McGraw-Hill, 1971.

Schlesinger, Arthur, Jr. *A Thousand Days: John F. Kennedy in the White House*. Greenwich: Fawcett Crest, 1965.

Sharkansky, Ira, ed. *Policy Analysis in Political Science*. Chicago: Markham, 1970.

Somers, Gerald, ed. *Retraining the Unemployed*. Madison: University of Wisconsin Press, 1968.

——, and Donald Woods, eds. *Cost-Benefit Analysis of Manpower Policies*. Kingston, Ont.: Industrial Relations Centre, Queens University, 1969.

Sorensen, Theodore. *Kennedy*. New York: Bantam Books, 1965.

Steiner, Gilbert. *The State of Welfare*. Washington, D.C.: The Brookings Institution, 1971.

Sundquist, James. *Making Federalism Work*. Washington, D.C.: The Brookings Institution, 1969.

——. *Politics and Policy: The Eisenhower, Kennedy and Johnson Years*. Washington, D.C.: The Brookings Institution, 1968.

——, ed. *On Fighting Poverty*. New York: Basic Books, 1969.

Thompson, Wilbur. *A Preface to Urban Economics*. Baltimore: The Johns Hopkins Press, 1968.

Thurnstrom, Stephen. *Poverty, Planning and Politics in the New Boston: The Origins of ABCD*. New York: Basic Books, 1969.

Thurow, Lester. *Poverty and Discrimination*. Washington, D.C.: The Brookings Institution, 1969.

Truman, David. *The Governmental Process*. New York: Alfred A. Knopf, 1960.

Waxman, Chaim, ed. *Poverty: Power and Politics*. New York: Grosset & Dunlap, 1968.

Weissman, Harold, ed. *Community Development in the Mobilization for Youth Experience*. New York: Association Press, 1969.

White, Theodore. *The Making of the President, 1960*. New York: Atheneum, 1961.

Wholey, Joseph, *et al. Federal Evaluation Policy*. Washington, D.C.: The Urban Institute, 1970.

Wilson, James, ed. *City Politics and Public Policy*. New York: John Wiley & Sons, 1968.

ARTICLES

Bachrach, Peter, and Morton Baratz. "Decisions and Nondecisions: An Analytic Framework," *American Political Science Review* 57, 3 (September 1963), 641-51.

——. "A Power Analysis: The Shaping of Anti-Poverty Policy in Baltimore," *Public Policy* 18, 2 (Winter 1970), 155-86.

——. "Two Faces of Power," *American Political Science Review* 56, 4 (December, 1962), 947-52.

Banfield, Edward, and James Wilson. "Public Regardingness as a Value Premise in Voting Behavior," *American Political Science Review* 57, 4 (December 1964), 876-87.

Bay, Christian. "Politics and Pseudopolitics: A Critical Evaluation of Some Behavioral Literature," *American Political Science Review* 59, 2 (March 1965).

Borus, Michael. "A Benefit-Cost Analysis of the Economic Effectiveness of Retraining the Unemployed," *Yale Economic Essays* 4 (Fall 1964), pp.371-430.

Cepuran, Joseph. "CAP Expenditures in the Fifty States: A Comparison," *Urban Affairs Quarterly*, March 1969, pp. 325-41.

Cnudde, Charles, and Donald McCrone. "Party Competition and Welfare Policies in the American States," *American Political Science Review* 63, 3 (September 1969), 858-66.

121

Dawson, Richard, and James Robinson. "Interparty Competition, Economic Variables and Welfare Policies in the American States," *Journal of Politics* 25 (May 1963), pp. 265-89.

Dye, Thomas. "Income, Inequality and American State Politics," *American Political Science Review* 63, 2 (March 1969), 157-62.

Frey, Fredrick. "Comment: On the Issues and Nonissues in the Study of Power," *American Political Science Review* 65, 4 (December 1971), 1081-1101.

Grove, Walter, and Herbert Costner. "Organizing the Poor: Evaluation of a Strategy," *Social Science Quarterly* 50, 3 (December 1969), 643-56.

Lineberry, Robert, and Edmund Fowler. "Reformism and Public Policies in American Cities," *American Political Science Review* 64, 3 (September 1967), 701-16.

MacDonald, Dwight. "Our Invisible Poor," The *New Yorker,* January 19, 1963, pp. 82-92.

Main, Earl. "A Nationwide Evaluation of MDTA Institutional Job Training," *Journal of Human Resources* 3, 2 (Spring 1968), 159-70.

March, James. "The Power of Power," in David Easton, ed., *Varieties of Political Theory.* Englewood Cliffs, N.J.: Prentice-Hall, 1966.

Marmor, Theodore. "On Comparing Income Maintenance Alternatives," *American Political Science Review* 65, 1 (March 1971), 83-96.

Merelman, Richard. "On the Neoelitist Critique of Community Power," *American Political Science Review* 62, 2 (June 1968), 451-60.

Orshansky, Mollie. "Counting the Poor: Another Look at the Poverty Profile," *Social Security Bulletin,* January 1965, pp. 2-29.

Page, David. "Retraining Under the Manpower Development Training Act: A Cost-Benefit Analysis," *Public Policy* 13, pp. 257-67.

Petersen, Paul. "Forms of Representation: Participation of the Poor in the Community Action Program," *American Political Science Review* 64, 2 (June 1970), 491-507.

Pious, Richard. "Policy and Public Administration: The Legal Services Program in the War on Poverty," *Politics and Society* 1, 3 (May 1971), 365-92.

Rein, Martin, and Robert Weiss. "The Evaluation of Broad-Aim Programs: A Cautionary Case and a Moral," *Annals,* September 1969, pp. 133-42.

Schick, Allen. "The Road to PPB: The Stages of Budget Reform," *Public Administration Review* 26, December 1966, pp. 243-58.

Sharkansky, Ira, and Richard Hofferbert. "Dimensions of State Politics, Economics and Public Policy," *American Political Science Review* 63, 3 (September 1969), 867-79.

Sheppard, Harold. "Some Broader Reality Frameworks for Antipoverty Intervention," *Social Science Quarterly* 50, 3 (December 1969), 487-93.

122

Somers, Gerald, and Ernst Stromsdorfer. "Benefit-Cost Analysis of Manpower Retraining," *Proceedings of the 17th Annual Meeting,* Industrial Relations Research Association, (Madison, Wis., 1965), pp. 172-85.

Stromsdorfer, Ernst. "Determinants of Economic Success in Retraining the Unemployed," *Journal of Human Resources* (Spring 1968), pp. 139-58.

Walker, Jack. "A Critique of the Elitist Theory of Democracy," *American Political Science Review* 60, 2 (June 1966), 285-95.

Witte, Edwin. "Administrative Agencies and Statute Lawmaking," *Public Administration Review* 2, 2 (March 1942).

Wolfinger, Raymond. "Nondecisions in the Study of Local Politics," *American Political Science Review* 75, 4 (December 1971), 1063-80.

GOVERNMENT DOCUMENTS

Advisory Commission on Intergovernmental Relations. *Intergovernmental Relations in the Poverty Program.* A Commission Report. Washington, D.C., April 1966.

Economic Report of the President, Washington, D.C., January 1964.

National Advisory Commission on Civil Disorders, *Report.* Washington, D.C., 1968.

President's Commission on Income Maintenance Programs. *Poverty Amid Plenty: The American Paradox.* Washington, D.C., 1969.

Public Papers of the Presidents of the United States, Lyndon B. Johnson. Washington, D.C., 1964, 1968, and 1969.

U.S. Bureau of the Census, *Current Population Reports.* "Income in 1971 of Families and Persons in the United States." Washington, D.C., 1972.

——. *Current Population Reports.* "Characterisitcs of the Low Income Population, 1970." Washington, D.C., 1971.

U.S. Congress. House. Committee on Appropriations. Subcommittee on Departments of Labor, Health, Education, and Related Agencies. *Department of Labor Appropriations,* for fiscal years 1963 through 1971. Hearings. 87th Cong., 2d sess. through 91st Cong. 2d sess.

——. *Office of Economic Opportunity Appropriations,* for fiscal years 1965 through 1971. Hearings. 88th Cong., 2d Sess. through 91st Cong., 2d Sess.

U.S. Congress. House. Committee on Education and Labor. Select Labor Subcommittee. *Manpower Development and Training Act of 1962* and *Amendments* of 1963, 1965, 1966, and 1968. Hearings. 87th Cong., 2d sess.; 88th Cong., 1st sess.; 89th Cong., 1st and 2d sessions; 90th cong., 2d sess.

——. *Manpower Act of 1969.* Hearings. 91st Cong., 1st and 2d sessions.

U.S. Congress. House. Committee on Education and Labor. Subcommittee on the War on Poverty. *Economic Opportunity Act of 1964* and *Amendments* of 1965 and 1966. Hearings. 88th Cong., 2d sess.; 89th Cong., 1st and 2d sessions.

U.S. Congress. Joint Economic Committee. Subcommittee on Economy in Government. *The Analysis and Evaluation of Public Expenditures.* A Compendium of Papers. 91st Cong., 1st sess., 1969.

U.S. Congress. Joint Economic Committee. Subcommittee on Fiscal Policy. *The Effectiveness of Manpower Training Programs: A Review of the Research on the Impact on the Poor.* Staff Study. 92d Cong., 2d sess., 1972.

U.S. Congress. Senate. Committee on Labor and Public Welfare. Subcommittee on Employment, Manpower, and Poverty. *Economic Opportunity Act of 1964* and *Amendments* of 1965, 1966, and 1969. Hearings. 88th Cong., 1st and 2d sessions; 89th Cong., 1st and 2d sessions; 91st Cong., 1st sess.

——. *Examination of the War on Poverty.* Hearings, Staff and Consultant Reports. 90th Cong., 1st sess., 1967.

——. *Manpower Development and Training Act of 1962* and *Amendments* of 1963, 1965, 1966, and 1968. Hearings. 87th Cong., 2d sess.; 88th Cong., 1st sess.; 89th Cong., 1st and 2d sessions; 90th Cong., 2d sess.

——. *Manpower Development and Training Legislation, 1970.* Hearings. 91st Cong., 1st and 2d sessions.

——. *Nation's Manpower Revolution.* Hearings. 88th Cong., 1st and 2d sessions, 1963-64.

U.S. Congress. Senate. Special Committee on Unemployment Problems. *Hearings, Studies in Unemployment, Readings in Unemployment,* and *Report 1206.* 86th Cong., 2d sess., 1960.

U.S. Department of Health, Education, and Welfare. *Annual Report to Congress on Training Activities Under the Manpower Development and Training Act* (various titles). 1963 through 1971.

——. *Toward a Social Report.* Washington, D.C., 1969.

U.S. Department of Labor. *Manpower Report of the President.* Washington, D.C., 1963 through 1972.

——. *Neighborhood Youth Corps: A Review of Research.* Manpower Administration Research Monograph No. 13. Washington, D.C., 1970.

U.S. Office of Economic Opportunity, Community Action Program. *Annual Report* (various titles). 1964 through 1969.

——. *Community Action Program Guide.* 1965.

GOVERNMENT-SPONSORED RESEARCH STUDIES

Barss, Reitzel, and Associates, Inc. "Attributes of Successful Community Action Programs," Cambridge, Mass., March 1968.

———. "Community Action and Institutional Change," Cambridge, Mass., July 1969.

———. "Community Action and Urban Institutional Change," Cambridge, Mass., August 1970.

———. "The Impact of the Community Action Programs on Institutional Change: Assistance to Community Organizations as a Successful Strategy," Cambridge, Mass., May 1970.

———. "Mobilizing Poor Communities," Cambridge, Mass., 1970.

Daniel Yankelovich, Inc. "A Study of the Effects of Sections 210 and 211 of the 1967 Amendments of the EOA as Required Under Section 233(c) of the Amendments," New York, February 1969.

———. "A Study of the Nonprofessional in the Community Action Program," New York, September 1966.

Decision Making Information. "MDTA Outcomes Study: Final Report," Santa Ana, Cal., November 1971.

National Opinion Research Center. "Community Action Programs as Agents of Change in the Private Welfare Sector," Chicago, August 1969.

———. "Community Mobilization and Institutional Change: The Influence of the CAP in Large Cities," Chicago, August 1969.

———. "Community Organization Efforts, Political and Institutional Change, and the Diffusion of Change Produced by Community Action Programs," Chicago, April 1970.

———. "National Evaluation of Urban Community Action Programs," Chicago, June 1969.

———. "A Nationwide Evaluation of MDTA Institutional Job Training Programs," Chicago, 1967.

Olympus Research Corporation. "Total Impact Evaluation of Manpower Programs in Four Cities," Washington, D.C., August 1971.

School of Labor and Industrial Relations, Michigan State University. "Economic Benefits and Costs of Retraining Courses in Michigan," East Lansing, December 1969.

———. "Retraining Under the MDTA: A Study of Attributes of Trainees Associated with Successful Retraining," East Lansing, 1970.

Systems Development Corp. "Evaluation of the JOBS Program in Nine Cities," Falls Church, Va., September 1969.

125

OTHER SOURCES

Ball, Joseph H. "The Implementation of Federal Manpower Policy: A Study of Bureau-cratic Competition and Intergovernmental Relations." Unpublished Ph.D. dissertation, Department of Political Science, Columbia University, 1972.

Eisenger, Peter. "The Antipoverty Community Action Group as a Political Force in the Ghetto." Unpublished Ph.D. dissertation, Department of Political Science, Yale University, 1969.

Hoffman, Richard Lee. "Community Action: Innovative and Coordinative Strategies in the War on Poverty." Unpublished Ph.D. dissertation, Department of Political Science, University of North Carolina, 1968.

Smith, Brian. "The Role of the Poor in the Poverty Program: The Origin and Development of Maximum Feasible Participation." Unpublished Master's thesis, Department of Public Law and Government, Columbia University, 1966.

CHARLES BRECHER has been a Research Associate at the Conservation of Human Resources Project since 1968. He holds a Ph.D. in Political Science from the City University of New York (1973) and a B.A. degree with Honors from the University of Florida (1965). He is the author of *Upgrading Blue Collar and Service Workers* (Baltimore: The Johns Hopkins Press, 1972) and a coauthor of two books by Eli Ginzberg and the Conservation of Human Resources Staff, *Urban Health Services: The Case of New York* (New York: Columbia University Press, 1971) and *New York Is Very Much Alive: A Manpower View* (New York: McGraw-Hill, 1973).

OTHER CONSERVATION OF HUMAN RESOURCES STUDIES—
COLUMBIA UNIVERSITY

EMPLOYMENT EXPANSION AND METROPOLITAN TRADE

Richard Victor Knight

THE LABOR MARKET: AN INFORMATION SYSTEM

Boris Yavitz, Dean W. Morse, with Anna B. Dutka

UNEMPLOYMENT IN THE URBAN CORE
An Analysis of Thrity Cities with Policy Recommendations

Stanley L. Friedlander, assisted by Robert Shick